What Price

Economic Growth?

What Price

Economic Growth?

Edited by

KLAUS KNORR *and* WILLIAM J. BAUMOL

Contributors

WILLIAM J. BAUMOL
STERIE T. BEZA
WILLIAM G. BOWEN
WILLIAM CARMICHAEL
KLAUS KNORR
JESSE MARKHAM
GARDNER PATTERSON
RICHARD E. QUANDT
SIDNEY VERBA

A SPECTRUM  BOOK

PRENTICE-HALL, INC.

Library of Congress
Catalog Card No.: 61:13344

PRINTED IN THE UNITED STATES OF AMERICA

95500-C

Preface

Early in 1959, we became keenly interested in the growing public discussion of the growth performance of the American economy in the 1950's and its ability to sustain American security over the longer run in view of the persistently higher rates of economic growth in the Soviet Bloc. We were disturbed by the fact that, though numerous groups were willing enough to advocate a speeding up of our economic growth, there seemed to be a remarkable paucity of concrete and detailed proposals for accomplishing this aim and little analysis of the social costs which would be involved.

We were fortunate in being able to persuade some of our colleagues at Princeton to collaborate on a pilot study. At our first meeting, held in April 1959, it was decided to examine, by way of illustration, the consequences of a particular scheme, originally formulated by one of the editors, which was designed to effect a substantial acceleration of American economic growth without generating inflationary pressures and without necessitating direct controls or detailed governmental regulation of the economy. The group agreed to hold seminar meetings about once a month and to prepare first drafts of papers during the summer. These papers were discussed in the fall and revised during the winter.

The authors are grateful to several other colleagues who met with the group and gave it their criticism and advice. They were Professors Lester V. Chandler, Ansley J. Coale, Fritz Machlup, and Paul Strayer. The authors are especially indebted to Professor Edgar O. Edwards, now at Rice University, who wrote a discerning and critical appraisal of the Baumol proposal.

The Center of International Studies at Princeton provided financial support for the study. During the summer of 1960, the work of Professors Markham and Quandt was supported by funds supplied by a Ford Foundation grant to the Department of Economics.

Klaus Knorr and William J. Baumol

Princeton, New Jersey

Contents

vii

4

The Fiscal Structure of the Proposal •

WILLIAM D. CARMICHAEL   48

5

Measurement of the Effectiveness of the Tax-

Subsidy Plan • RICHARD E. QUANDT   62

6

Implications of Growth Incentives for the

Problems of Inflation and Unemployment •

WILLIAM G. BOWEN   74

7

Growth Incentives and Antitrust Policy •

8

Economic Expansion, External Solvency, and

the Gains from Trade • STERIE T. BEZA AND

9

Some Political Obstacles to the Implementation

of Economic Growth Proposals • SIDNEY VERBA

What Price
Economic Growth?

· 1 ·

Purposes of an
Accelerated Growth Program

KLAUS KNORR

The campaign for the Presidential election in 1960 was, among other things, remarkable for the attention which both candidates paid to the requirements of national security and foreign policy. Within this context, both candidates referred repeatedly to the prospective growth of the American economy. In the fall of 1960, in fact, this was no longer a new theme, for the growth performance of the American economy had for several years provoked sharp and increasing public controversy.

Demands for faster economic growth have been voiced in many and various quarters. It is clear that this excitement has been aroused by a gathering anxiety over the security of the United States, and of the West as a whole, based on concern over whether or not it can be safeguarded in the longer run in the face of greater rates of economic growth in the Sino-Soviet bloc, and especially in the Soviet Union.

This concern has been based predominantly on the fear of two contingencies: first, the abiding hostility of communist leaders to the political and economic organization of the western societies and, second, the increasing capability with which high rates of economic growth may enable the communist bloc to implement their hostile intentions, in contrast with the

United States which, it has often been asserted, cannot afford to increase substantially its outlays on national security lest its economy be subverted by the burden. In the 1960 campaign, President Kennedy highlighted the connection between American economic growth and American security. Thus, on November 1, he said: ". . . unless we are moving here at home, we cannot move the cause of freedom around the world. If we lack a first rate growing economy, we cannot maintain a first rate defense."[1] And a few days later he stated that, unless new policies in science, military and economic strength are pursued, the Soviet Union will be ahead by 1970 in all three categories. "How many countries will follow a leader who is not able to maintain his lead?"[2]

The authors of the present study became interested in this problem for two reasons. On grounds which we will shortly explain, we associate ourselves (despite some reservations) with the widespread worries about the economic foundations of our national security. And, given this uneasiness, we deplore the absence of analyses which throw light both on policy measures through which American economic growth could be appreciably accelerated, and on the costs, by which we mean the entire range of undesirable consequences, including non-economic burdens, which their implementation would impose on American society.[3] A comparison of the national security risks

---

[1] *The New York Times,* November 1, 1960, p. 29.

[2] *Ibid,* November 7, 1960, p. 28.

[3] A considerable literature on accelerated economic growth in the United States has been accumulating during the last few years. Much of this is in the form of speeches and brief papers and reports which advocate or discuss different assortments of growth policies and undoubtedly make interesting points and, often, wise observations. However, they cannot be expected, and were not intended, to analyze rigorously the consequences of the specific or general remedies proposed. Among these are: Rockefeller Brothers Fund, *The Challenge to America: Its Economic and Social Aspects* (New York, 1958); Chamber of Commerce of the United States, *The Promise of Economic Growth* (Washington, D.C., 1960);

of relatively slow economic growth with the costs of acceleration and a forecast of the distribution of these costs are prerequisite to a sensible decision. Obviously, if the security risks were very high, we would be willing to bear considerable costs in order to reduce them, though there would always be limits to the price we care to pay. Conversely, the aggregate costs, as defined, might be so painful that we would be prepared to run even the most dangerous security risks.

Committee for Economic Development, *The Budget and Economic Growth* (1959); American Federation of Labor and Congress of Industrial Organizations, *Policies for Economic Growth* (Washington, D.C., 1959); Leon H. Keyserling, "Next Step—A 600 Billion Dollar Economy?" *The New York Times Magazine,* November 23, 1958; Sumner H. Slichter, "Argument for 'Creeping' Inflation," *The New York Times Magazine,* March 8, 1959; Charles E. Silberman and Sanford S. Parker, "How The U.S. Can Get 50 Per Cent Richer," *Fortune,* LIX (March, 1959), pp. 107-113, 199; and the series of White House releases formulated by the Cabinet Committee on Price Stability for Economic Growth in 1960.

The National Planning Association has published several excellent reports, e.g., *Long-Range Projections for Economic Growth: The American Economy in 1970,* and *The Economy of the American People: Progress, Problems, Prospects.* But the references to particular growth policies are brief. This is true of much of the contribution made by professional economists, e.g., the several papers presented at the 1959 meeting of the American Economic Association, published in *Papers and Proceedings, American Economic Review,* L (May, 1960).

In some ways the richest sources are the volumes of hearings and reports published by Joint Economic Committee, Congress of the United States, 86th Congress, under the general title, *Employment, Growth and Price Levels* (Washington, D.C.: Government Printing Office). These volumes contain valuable papers on the history of economic growth in the United States but, partly because this effort was primarily concerned with the reconciliation of growth and stability, the bulk of the analysis is preoccupied with stability rather than economic growth. To take the hearings of October 26-30, 1959, as an example, of the eight economists involved—Professors Musgrave, Baumol, Machlup, Hart, Triffin, Gordon, Heller and Friedman—only Baumol's focus is on economic growth. Several of the others express skepticism toward any deliberate policy aimed at acceleration of American economic output and, incidentally, do so on grounds regarding which, as economists, they lack an expert's qualification. Such positive growth proposals as are made, appear in the form of dicta.

1. Soviet and American rates of growth. We realize that comparisons of Soviet and American rates of economic growth suffer from several controversial technical problems. These we wish to side-step, not because they are uninteresting, but because we have chosen a different focus for our effort. Thus, we agree that aggregate changes in the real Gross National Product (GNP) over time, either in absolute volume or per capita, do not afford a wholly satisfactory measurement of economic growth. However, as a rough approximation, we think this measure good enough for our purpose. We also know that estimates of the Soviet and American GNP's and of their growth, and comparisons between them, are highly controversial, these again for good reasons. We simply assume that the large majority of experts are not far wrong in claiming that, during the 1950's, the Soviet GNP grew at a rate about twice as fast as the American.

Choosing, somewhat arbitrarily, the estimates of the Central Intelligence Agency, we start with the finding that, during the 1950's, the real GNP is estimated to have increased at an average of $3\frac{1}{4}$ per cent per year in the United States, and at an average of 7 per cent in the USSR. Over the same period, industrial production is estimated to have expanded by an average of 4 per cent in the United States, and 10 per cent in the Soviet Union.[4] For the United States plus its allies and the Soviet Union and its satellites, the respective growth rates were estimated at averages of 4 and $7\frac{1}{2}$ per cent for GNP's and of $4\frac{3}{4}$ and $10\frac{1}{2}$ per cent for industrial production.[5]

On the difficult technical problems encountered in compar-

----

[4] *Comparisons of the United States and Soviet Economies.* Prepared by the Central Intelligence Agency in Cooperation with the Department of State and the Department of Defense for the Subcommittee on Economic Statistics of the Joint Economic Committee, Congress of the United States, 86th Congress, 2d Session, Washington, 1960, pp. 48-49.

[5] *Ibid.*

ing GNP's and their expansion there is a large and competent literature to be consulted. There are, however, a number of other objections and queries that have been levelled against the proponents of more rapid economic growth in the United States. Because these arguments deal with predictions, or intangibles, or are incapable of rigorous analysis, we feel that we should indicate where we stand regarding them, and how we arrived at our serious concern over the growth performance of the American economy. Like most proponents of accelerated economic growth, we favor it for national security reasons,[6] and, even in this respect, only to prepare the United States to meet certain contingencies which, even though they may never occur, have a considerable probability of arising. We are not interested in making a fetish of economic growth. We definitely would feel no cause for alarm over the American growth performance during the 1950's if the United States lived in a peaceful world. But we do not live in such a world. We are inclined to take seriously Mr. Khrushchev's threat that the Communists will "bury" us. Despite ups and downs in the acrimony of the East-West conflict, and in overt Soviet aggressiveness, there is no good evidence that the communist leaders do not mean what they say. They believe the capitalist system to be doomed, and they are working actively to hasten its demise, though not necessarily by military means.

The hope is sometimes expressed that the communist commitment to world revolution will weaken over time, and eventually perhaps cease altogether, thus permitting a more amicable state of world affairs, which would obviate any concern

---

[6] We recognize that faster economic growth in the United States is sometimes also desired for non-security purposes. This is obviously a legitimate desire, but it is very questionable whether this purpose is worth the social costs which would be involved in a substantial growth program.

over dangers to national security resulting from rapid economic expansion in the communist camp. This may, of course, happen. The social, political, and cultural systems of the Soviet Union are in fact in a noticeable process of change, and such changes are bound to be pronounced when a society becomes industrialized at such a ruthless speed. It is even plausible that the achievement and fruits of economic growth will profoundly modify the preferences of Soviet society and, from this point of view, rapid economic growth in the communist countries is perhaps to be welcomed rather than deplored. However, predictions about changes in Soviet society and its values, and about the direction and speed of these changes, are far too hazardous to dissipate our anxieties. We do know that such structural changes need considerable time to mature, requiring generations, or at least decades, rather than years.

There are also predictions that the rate of economic growth in the Soviet Union will be slowing down appreciably and, in contrast, that the American rate will become higher automatically—the implication being that the recent differences in growth rates will wane. There are several grounds on which one would expect the productivity of Soviet capital investment to fall, that is, the declining fund of advanced technology which can be "borrowed" from abroad, the depletion of the richest and most accessible mineral deposits, the pressing need to invest heavily in housing and other sectors with a relatively high capital-output ratio. Indeed the time may soon come, in less than ten years perhaps, when further accumulation of capital in the Soviet Union at the speed of recent years will no longer make sense, and a larger proportion of resources will be diverted to consumption. Yet the Communists may develop innovations in products, production techniques, economic organization, etc., which will tend to raise the efficiency of investment and thus offset the countervailing tendencies in part, or perhaps entirely for a time. Even if Soviet growth rates were to decline gradually but slowly, it would take a good many years before the current gap would be narrowed to an acceptable size. But, again, the crucial fact is that prediction on this matter is precarious. Similarly, the statement of *Fortune* magazine that because the American labor force will be growing faster in the 1960's, and because productivity ". . . has been rising at 3 per cent a year since World War II . . ." the national growth rate "should add up" to 4.25 per cent a year,[7] is a prognostication. A forecast of the expansion in the labor force may be quite safe, but the rise in man-hours actually worked is more difficult to predict, and so is the rise in productivity.

To conclude, we think that we should provide for contingencies whose probability is unknown but certainly not minute, and whose consequences would be extremely serious, as long as there are acceptable alternatives to undue risk taking.

2. Significance of growth rates and output structure. But do these differences in the rates of economic growth really matter? The need to make predictions in the face of uncertainty is again encountered in any serious attempt to answer this question. We believe the chances are that these differences do matter and that they may threaten the ability of the United States to survive in a hostile world. It is necessary to present our reasoning in some detail, for the ways in which these differences may matter is also highly relevant for the required composition of any accelerated GNP. The rationale of a deliberate speeding up of economic growth in the United States depends crucially on whether national security considerations call for more rapid growth with a very particular composition of out-

---

[7] *Fortune* (April, 1959), p. 99.

put, or can be satisfied by more rapid growth, which is within wide limits, independent of output composition.

As the world is currently organized, a country's ability to influence other countries depends substantially on the performance of its economy and on the allocation of economic resources to national security activities. We shall briefly discuss these relationships under four headings:[8] system reputation, foreign aid and investment, foreign trade, and defense.

Two points, however, need to be made beforehand:

First, because of the revolutionary change in weapons technology, national security depends now, far more than before the last world war, on current and sustained "peacetime" allocation of resources to these purposes rather than on the economic potential to make huge and sudden increases in military production and manpower immediately before or after the outbreak of war. Because the new weapons have virtually reduced the protective functions of time and space to zero, national military security rests primarily on ready, mobilized capabilities. This is not to say that economic war *potential,* in which the communist states are still decidedly, though decreasingly, inferior to the United States and its allies, is of no further importance; it would be critical in a large-scale and prolonged limited war; but the premium on mobilized military strength has risen immensely.

Second, the Soviet Union devotes to foreign policy and military purposes an appreciably larger proportion of its resources than does the United States or the West as a whole. It has been estimated by some experts that, though the USSR currently generates a national product somewhat less than half

---

[8] We neglect other national security activities, e.g. diplomacy, propaganda, and visitor exchanges, because their demands on economic resources are relatively small.

that of the United States, its military output, calculated at American prices, approximates that of the United States in absolute terms.[9] If these estimates are not far wrong, the Soviet Union (and the communist bloc) will be able to bring sharply increasing pressure to bear on the West if it maintains superior rates of economic growth and continues to allot a larger proportion of its output to foreign policy and military purposes.[10]

3. System reputation. The term "system reputation" refers to the image of the performance of the American economy (and, indirectly, of the American political, social, and cultural arrangements) as evaluated in the minds of foreigners in terms of *their own* values. A system's reputation rests on all kinds of performances which affect a nation's ability to satisfy wants; it is affected by instability, underemployment of resources, and so on. However, in a world which has become remarkably sensitive to economic development, growth performance has come to be a major factor in this evaluation. The communist world is systematically nursing this sensitivity and exploiting it by holding up the communist system as a model of superior performance. Since the rate of economic progress is widely taken as a general index of national vitality, efficiency, and capacity for survival, the Cold War has in part turned into a war of different economic and political systems, and system reputation has become a determinant of international loyalties and alli-

---

[9] Cf. the summary of a study prepared for the Army by the Operations Research Office of the Johns Hopkins University in *The New York Times,* November 6, 1960, p. 69.

[10] According to the ORO study, "If the U.S. and the U.S.S.R. continue to budget for defense in accordance with recent allocation patterns, by 1970 the respective budgets would be $46,000,000,000 for the U.S. and $72,000,000,000 for the U.S.S.R. (in 1959 dollar equivalents)." *Ibid.*

ance potential as well as a factor in domestic political and economic change, especially in the economically less developed countries.

At present it looks as if international system reputation is heavily affected by success in a statistical growth race and that composition of output is only of secondary importance. To the extent that composition does matter, its role is impossible to generalize or predict for we simply lack adequate information. To some foreign publics, a rich stream of consumers' goods and services, or some range of them, may matter more than, say, the construction of new steel mills and aluminum plants. Some publics may be especially sensitive to "cultural" output and may appreciate beauty of architecture and productivity in the arts much more than a hectic sequence of style changes in passenger automobiles. Others may place a high value on the absence of urban slums and an abundance of schools and hospitals, while still others are impressed by a plethora of bombers and missiles. Scientific progress and technological innovations appear to be widely esteemed. No doubt, the Soviet Union will challenge the United States from time to time in a particular line of output and attempt to make this challenge known in the rest of the world. Occasionally we may thereby be put under pressure, although that is not to say that, in this particular duel, we must always leave the choice of weapons to our opponent.

To conclude, it appears at this juncture that a favorable system reputation can be achieved in large part by rapid economic growth, by conspicuous scientific and technological progress, which is in any case a prerequisite of rapid economic growth, by a flexible economy which can achieve rapid, even though moderate, changes in output composition, and by the absence of large-scale unemployment.

4. Foreign economic aid. In view of the preoccupation of underdeveloped communities with rapid economic progress, or rather perhaps with its fruits, the various obstacles to their economic expansion, the expectation of receiving foreign aid, and increasing communist offers of assistance, the American capacity and willingness to give such aid and invest abroad are patently important. They are an indispensable asset in the international influence game, and in affecting the direction of political development as well as the nature and speed of economic growth in the less developed areas.

Other factors remaining the same, our capacity and, as will be argued below, our willingness to invest and make gifts abroad tend to grow with an expansion of our national product. Foreign aid and investment do not, however, require any *detailed* planning of output composition. Larger foreign expenditures on American goods and services, occasioned by our aid activities, will call forth the necessary reallocation of productive resources in the United States.

To say this is not to advocate a large or indiscriminate expansion of foreign aid. But we must be concerned with the American capacity to step up these activities should national security considerations recommend it.

5. International trade. The external position of the United States will also be strengthened by the provision of ample market opportunities to underdeveloped countries and to our more industrialized allies. It can be taken for granted that the American market will tend to become the more capacious, the faster the growth of our GNP. This effect is automatic, unless obstructed by trade policy, and does not, of course, require any particular composition of output, although certain types of output, such as services, require far smaller amounts of imported inputs than do other kinds of product, for example, automobiles.

For the United States to make large and continuous expenditures on foreign aid and for military purposes abroad—important national security requirements—it needs export- and import-competing industries capable of bringing about a substantial export surplus to match these external outlays over time, and maintain substantial reserves of international financial liquidity. *This* requirement may not be met by just any structure of output. As is concluded in Chapter 8, the mere acceleration of national output, regardless of structure, has an impact on the balance of payments which is difficult to predict, and it may very well result in a strain on the balance. But it is in the nature of our economic system that this problem, should it arise, will not call for the restructuring of national output by Government intervention. What we need, rather, is a national output which adapts readily to shifts in demand and comparative production advantages and a fiscal and monetary policy which minimizes inflation. The bringing about of changes in output composition must be left to our export- and import-competing industries.

6. Military preparation. It will be argued below that accelerated economic growth would benefit the American capacity and willingness to increase defense and defense-related Government expenditures, should our security position require it.

It is true that we would clearly prefer a particular composition of output if we needed to prepare for a war of a type like that of World Wars I and II. These wars of attrition were fought predominantly by means of equipment produced after the outbreak of hostilities, thus putting a peacetime premium on economic war potential; such potential depended chiefly on the prevalence of war-supporting industries and on productive facilities that could quickly be converted to, and expanded for, military production. However, the experts generally agree that such a war is now improbable (the United States has, in any case, an immense economic potential for large-scale and prolonged wars of attrition).

The more probable kinds of war are, first, all-out nuclear hostilities and, second, so-called "limited wars."

The deterrence or waging of all-out thermonuclear war requires military capability-in-being. (Even if a broken-back war continued after the exchange of nuclear blows, its demands on the devastated economy would have to be extremely minor, and its conduct, therefore, would also have to be based primarily on stocks.)

Here we come to the crucial point in our position on the means for achieving the desired composition of output. Any military or related requirements as to output composition involve primarily the nature of the goods produced for the public sector, and not the commodities made for private consumers or business firms. *But surely private enterprise can be relied upon to produce the goods required by the Government,* and to meet both quantity and quality specifications, *if the Government expenditures go up appropriately,* and its procurement is conducted with reasonable care. After all, business takes its markets where it can find them. If there is a brisk demand for military equipment (or, for that matter, for research or educational facilities), management can be relied upon to alter the composition of output to whatever extent is required. This is particularly so if at the same time a counter-inflationary program keeps private consumption demands sufficiently in check to make the required resources available to the public sector of the economy. In sum, in our view the achievement of an appropriate composition of output requires only two concomitant measures on the part of the Government: a sufficient increase in its outlays, and a suitable check on total consumption expenditures (but with absolutely no restriction on the composition of the latter). Thus, our answer to the question, "Would you be willing to see economic growth consist partly of frills and conspicuous consumption?" is a categorical "Yes." Indeed, with the accelerated rate of obsolescence in weapons systems, one would want an armaments industry which adapts its output rapidly to changes in military requirements. And to some extent, rapid adaptation is facilitated by "artificial" obsolescence of consumer goods and the willingness to adapt readily to consumer whims which is so characteristic of the American economy.

To turn to another aspect of military preparedness, the United States has thus far done extremely little to increase its capacity for recuperating from nuclear devastation, should such a disaster occur. However, if the United States wanted to do more in this direction, for example, by furnishing shelters, accumulating and storing stocks, building facilities for evacuated parts of the population, the resulting expenditures would also have to take place before the war and engender an automatic change in national output. Thus, once more the requisite change in composition of output calls only for a change in Government expenditures and a sufficient restriction of total private outlay.

So much for all-out nuclear hostilities. The alternative for which we must consider preparing ourselves is limited war, whose necessary characteristic is that it is limited in military objectives. It may likewise be limited in the employment of kinds of weapons systems, in the theatre and scale of operation and, perhaps less likely, in duration. These latter limitations will result from the natural fear that the relaxation of these limits will increase the risk of a spiralling of warfare and the chance that limited war will escalate to all-out war more or less by accident. However, the less vulnerable all-out war capabilities (that is, vehicles for delivery of nuclear bombs, and so on) are to a surprise attack, the less the chance of an accidental precipitation of all-out war, and hence the less likely the maintenance of any limitations other than limited objectives in the conduct of such a war. Since it is probable that all-out retaliatory systems will be fairly invulnerable by the mid-1960's, any limited war may involve large-scale and prolonged conflicts as well as small-scale and brief engagements (provided non-communist forces are strong enough to avert defeat in minor or brief actions).

Military experts are generally agreed that, largely because the Soviet bloc is maintaining large mobilized forces for surface warfare, limited war also requires the non-communist states to maintain highly mobilized (and for the United States highly mobile) forces for this purpose. However, for the reasons just indicated (and as has already happened during the Korean War), limited wars might be sufficiently large and prolonged to require limited mobilization and a speedy increase in the production of military manpower and goods (except to the extent that we maintain reserve military personnel and military stocks). In the case of the United States, this contingency again requires a capacity for rapid if moderate changes in the peacetime output structure. The problem is then one of converting productive facilities to a new pattern of demand. There is no good reason why that part of our capacity then required for military purposes should not have been previously employed in the manufacture of washing machines and television sets. Of course, to the extent that the United States in peacetime steps up its production of the goods which give it limited-war capabilities, a course of action recommended by many experts, this peacetime reallocation of resources would more directly improve the nation's preparedness for waging limited war.

The allocation of more resources to defense and for foreign-policy purposes would, of course, not by itself guarantee the security of the United States. These resources might be used inefficiently. Indeed, the level of efficiency in the formulation and implementation of national security policies is probably not very high anywhere in the world in view of the very great uncertainties involved in technological, military, political and morale decisions.[11] Nevertheless, it is reasonably certain that our security will be increased by an expansion in our military outlays. For a considerable range of effort well beyond that which is expended by governments today, the gains can be spectacular, for they can cover risks which have so far been left uncovered and in which the stakes involved are high. For instance, it is hardly necessary to stress the importance of rendering our nuclear retaliatory capability less vulnerable to surprise attack as soon as possible. Or the strengthening of our limited-war capability, which we have been reducing for reasons of economy, might obviate the need to choose sometime and somewhere between local surrender and being driven to the brink of all-out nuclear conflict.

7. The need for growth in GNP. But even though it be granted that the national security position of the United States might profit from an increased allocation of resources, it may be contended that this is a problem of re-allocating existing output and not one requiring that output expand

---

[11] Though we should of course strive to improve the management of resources allotted to national security, it is probably much more difficult to increase substantially the military value squeezed out of a typical unit of resource input than to increase the quantity of resources going into military uses.

faster than it has been. After all, the American GNP is still far larger than Soviet Russia's, and even though the American growth rate is appreciably below that of the USSR, we are presumably still adding to it each year a larger volume of goods and services than does the Soviet Union. Why then do we need faster economic growth in order to outspend our opponent? The question is reasonable, but only up to a point. There are limits to the extent to which the American public is prepared to be taxed more heavily for defense, foreign economic aid, and so forth. The evidence is somewhat ambiguous because the public's mettle has not been tested in recent years by a clear call for greater sacrifices from the country's leadership. However, the evidence of the longer past is one of chariness in peacetime and a willingness to take on large burdens only in time of war or dramatic crises. Such a fluctuating and mercurial response is, unfortunately, not good enough in a cold war which may well go on for decades, and in which a hot war is always a possibility.

Moreover, if the nation were to decide to devote persistently a larger proportion of its GNP to national security, which would certainly help in the shorter run, we might nevertheless in the longer run still find it increasingly difficult to counter the mounting pressure which the communist bloc could exert as a result of its superior rates of economic growth. The United States then might well have been better off if it had initially allocated more resources to economic growth.

In contrast, it is surely plausible that the American public is more likely to allocate additional resources to national security if its income should grow at a higher rate. We cannot be certain that this would happen, but it is plausible that it would.[12] If the need for high and rising outlays on national

---

[12] The argument that Americans have an unchangeably low peacetime marginal propensity to allocate part of their income to pay for their

security persists, and the nation's leadership recognizes and
acts vigorously on behalf of this need, there should be no
difficulty in maintaining the allocation of resources for these
purposes at the recent rate of about 10 per cent of the GNP.
The faster the real GNP expands, the more resources would
then be available for the national security sector. In fact, if
tax rates remain unchanged, and the pressure to reduce these
would be mitigated by rapidly growing personal incomes, tax
revenues would almost certainly increase at a higher rate than
the GNP as more taxpayers with rising incomes moved into
higher tax brackets. The Government would thus automatically be enabled to increase national security expenditures
more rapidly than the national income. Finally, it seems
plausible that the political acceptability of demands by the
nation's leadership for increased national security outlays will
rise with the rate at which the real private GNP expands.
Thus, although substantial increases in expenditures on national security do not follow automatically from substantial
increases in the real national income, it is not unrealistic to
expect political acceptance of larger national security expenditures as a consequence of faster economic growth. Appendix A further explores the relationship between growth of
national production and an increase in resources claimed by
the public sector.

---

country's national security is controverted by the historical record. During
the 1930's national security expenditures in the United States amounted
to little more than 1 per cent of the GNP. After the abandonment of the
isolationist position and the recognition of the international threat of
communism, these expenditures averaged around 10 per cent of the
GNP. Surely this is a significant change.

· 2 ·

A Family of Growth Proposals
and Their Costs

KLAUS KNORR

Even if the argument of Chapter 1 is accepted, it may still be reasonable to oppose any measures aimed at materially increasing economic growth in the United States on the ground that they require the nation to pay too stiff a price. There are such costs, and it is fair to assume that the faster economic growth proceeds, the greater will be the required costs. The problem is to separate necessary from unnecessary costs (there are choices of measures entailing different sets of costs) and to evaluate, eventually by the test of political acceptability, how heavily these costs weigh on the structure of American goals and preferences.

It is the purpose of this book to explore the range and magnitude of these costs. We do so chiefly by analyzing, as far as possible, the consequences of a particular scheme, presented in Chapters 3 and 4, for accelerating economic growth in the United States. However, we believe that the costs of any acceptable scheme would not differ substantially from those which we describe.

1. Unnecessary costs: inflation and regimentation. The opposition to accelerated economic growth in the United States emphasizes two kinds of costs which, in our opinion, are unnecessary. They are identified with the fears of inflation and of a vast extension of Government planning of, and control over, the economy.

We agree that any substantial increase in direct Government interference in the economy and any substantial degree of inflation are unpalatable on grounds of equity and efficiency. But we do not think that these costs need be paid. Thus, the particular growth scheme we examine is unlikely to add materially to the inflationary pressures already at work in the economy. To anticipate the analysis in Chapter 6, we are unable to predict the precise consequences of the growth scheme in this respect, but we are convinced that if it would occasionally generate net inflationary pressure, the amount would be small and could be counteracted by appropriate monetary and fiscal policies.

One method for speeding up a nation's economic growth is for Government authorities to decide on a high rate of savings and investment and to enforce these decisions on the community. This method, applied successfully in the Soviet Union, is incompatible with the American way of life which treasures the individual's freedom of choice. The growth scheme which we examine in considerable detail, and this would hold true of the entire family of similar schemes, requires no appreciable extensions of government control over the economy.

A central problem in this respect is whether we want faster economic growth in general, or whether we need and want more rapid growth only if it conforms to a specified structure of output and hence of productive capacity. As long as we want to accelerate economic growth for reasons of national security, it is extraordinarily fortunate that these reasons do not indicate any strong need for the enforcement of specific output patterns and hence no need for the pre-planning of output by public authority nor for the public imposition of these plans on the economy. If this were not so, if a particular output composition were important, we would be disposed to accept far greater national security risks than we should like to tolerate, for we would have little confidence in the ability of Government to predict the required output structure and to implement its plans. Furthermore, even if the Government commanded the necessary wisdom and administrative competence, we would find such a revolutionary transformation of American economic life, one which was not short-lived as during World War II but which would be needed for an indefinite future, highly obnoxious. The nation's present economic system is, after all, a vital part of the America which we want to make secure against external threat and interference. For this very reason, any method for accelerating economic growth should not interfere with free consumers' choice.

Faster growth is likely to lead to an increasing output of items which may seem frivolous to our sense of taste as individuals. We may even hope that a shift in values will, for example, generate more expenditures on making the United States a beautiful as well as a rich country. But a central characteristic of the community which we want to keep secure is the high value which it places on the individual's freedom to choose, even though we may not personally appreciate his tastes and even though, given his taste, he may make mistakes in exercising this choice.

The type of growth scheme we explore is designed to effect a rapid expansion of the nation's productive capacity. The scheme affects output composition almost entirely from the demand, not from the supply side. The structure of output would be left, as it is now, to the play of market demand; this means that the composition of output would vary automatically in response to changes on the demand side. Greater expenditures by Government on military products or education or slum clearance or by the foreign recipients of American economic aid, would assure the allocation of productive resources to these areas. Indeed, if the United States adopted a program of accelerated economic growth essentially for national security reasons, one would expect these kinds of expenditures to expand. Furthermore, if this were true, they would induce corresponding changes in the structure of output and productive capacity.

Although accelerating economic growth in the United States does not call for an extension of public control over the economy, we do believe that the stimulation of such growth does require changes in the agenda of public action. The particular scheme we discuss must be implemented through changes in established Government policy, especially tax policy, and we agree that the success of the scheme, and the minimization of undesirable side-effects, depend in some measure on supporting public action, which is indicated in the following chapters. Some modification of existing public policies would be required by any growth scheme of this kind.

2. *Necessary costs of accelerated economic growth.* Though inflation and regimentation are avoidable costs of faster growth, there are other and necessary costs of accelerating real economic expansion. Obviously, faster growth requires a higher rate of savings and investment, and the consumer must be induced to reduce his marginal consumption and the worker his claim for leisure below the level they would perhaps otherwise prefer. However, if output growth is accelerated sufficiently, there may be no need for consumption levels to fall over the long run; it would only mean that consumption must be decreased initially, and, over the longer run, even consumption might well rise more than it could have in the absence of growth stimulating policies. It is also possible that faster economic growth would, in part, come about through a longer average work week than would otherwise prevail but that this change would only mean a retardation in the secular trend toward increased leisure.

Accelerated economic growth means also that employers and workers would face more urgent pressures to adjust to changes in the demand for specific resources and bear the discomfort of these adjustments, which may be extremely painful to productive factors specific to, and localities specialized on, declining industries. And there would be more intangible costs, for example, the inconvenience to business management of having to adjust to changes in taxation, the effects of which could not easily be predicted. Thus, the particular growth scheme we discuss in detail would call for greater effort from business management. It would give a richer reward for superior effort, but it would also increase the penalty for inferior effort. It would diminish the relative security of reward, and this consequence might well be registered as an onerous cost to pay for faster economic growth. We are, of course, unable to measure these diverse costs. But there is no question that they are real. They and the other costs described in the following chapters are the price which must be paid for the benefits which faster economic expansion would confer on the community.

3. How high a rate of growth? How much acceleration of American economic growth should we strive for? We frankly do not know but assume that it should be appreciable. The optimum rate of growth would be one at which the gains from any further increase in growth would be equal to the costs as we have defined them; but no one can give operationally useful meaning to these terms. The only feasible method of settling this matter is by the test of political acceptability to what we hope will be a society which is reasonably well informed about the probable consequences of various choices. The authors of this book have concluded that, for the reasons stated, it is worth undertaking a study to examine whether the United States would be better off as the result of an appreciably more rapid rate of economic growth than it has enjoyed during the past decade. By "appreciable" we refer to a rate of growth which is perhaps roughly half again as high as the one the country has managed during the 1950's.

4. The focus of this study. The present study is sharply limited in focus, partly because the time which the authors were able to make available for it was restricted by other commitments, and partly because they feel that the growing public controversy on the need and merit of accelerated growth made it advantageous to offer a limited contribution as soon as possible rather than to publish a broader analysis in the more remote future.

In the first place, we decided to concentrate our study on the *method* of accelerating growth in the American economy. We did not begin, and could not have begun, with a broad-gauged exploration of the causes of, and obstacles to, economic growth. The fact is that empirical knowledge about the *ultimate* conditions of economic growth is fragmentary and slight, and the study of these basic conditions is largely outside the boundaries of economic expertise. We do not believe, however, that an increase in this knowledge is an indispensable prerequisite to the study of promoting growth. Its promotion can be properly studied in terms of *proximate* conditions. Analogously, the fact that there is little agreed knowledge of the ultimate causes of the business cycle has not been a handicap to the design of stabilization policies.

Our thinking about methods of acceleration has been governed by the criterion of compatibility with our basic economic and political system. We therefore rejected out of hand the method of regimentation applied in communist states. But if we want radically increased growth, there must be some radical change in the basis on which individuals and corporations make their decisions to save and invest, to innovate and manage resources.

In order to bring about such a radical change, two strategies could be contemplated. One is to rely chiefly on one decisive new measure; the other is to have recourse to relatively slight modifications of many existing policies in the hope that their cumulative effect would generate major results. We are inclined to favor the first alternative.

This approach is contrary to that of several proponents of more rapid economic growth who suggest that their objective can be approached by making a large variety of little changes in monetary and fiscal policies, in trade policy, in policy toward combinations of power in product and factor markets, in public investment, in education, patent legislation, in agricultural policy, and so forth.

Such proposals, though usually phrased vaguely, nevertheless merit serious analysis. Unfortunately, the efforts which the authors of the present study could undertake had to be limited and sharply focussed. We have not, therefore, studied the implications of the many proposals of that variety that have been made. We are sure that many of the small steps proposed could contribute to accelerated economic growth, and believe, indeed, that some of them come close to being indispensable to it. We suspect, however, that exclusive reliance on many little steps would not result in appreciably accelerated economic expansion; we suspect, furthermore, that it would not be easier politically to gain acceptance for a large number of little changes than for a radical measure upon which major reliance is placed.

5. A class of growth measures. Given the framework of our study, the desire to examine only thorough-going radical measures and our rejection of direct Government intervention in the economy, we believe we are left with only one family of possible proposals. If the Government is not to do the job, it must be left to private enterprise. And if private enterprise is not to be subjected to coercion, management must be supplied with tangible inducements to contribute to economic growth. Moreover, these inducements must not be directly selective, industry by industry and product by product, for this too would be tantamount to detailed central direction by the Government.

This, then, is the family of growth measures which remains to us—devices which somehow increase any individual business firm's rewards if it makes a contribution to economic growth. Many variants of such a policy nevertheless remain open. Accelerated depreciation or other subsidies to investment or a variety of other fiscal changes immediately suggest themselves.

In this volume we have, furthermore, limited ourselves to the fairly detailed examination of a growth scheme which is only one member of this group of possible radical measures. Thus, it would have been useful to explore in some detail the probable consequences of some other variants, or one which combined several of these measures. We will in fact offer some remarks on such alternatives, and believe that, through the study of one member of the class, we can learn a great deal about the entire family of radical measures.

In other words, we regard the particular scheme formulated by Professor Baumol in Chapter 3 as a prototype of all radical growth policies which are subject to the same kinds of constraints, especially the absence of Government regimentation and of inflationary finance for the promotion of growth. The advantage of closely examining this scheme lies in the relative specificity, thus far absent from the literature of recent growth proposals, with which its implications are spelled out in terms of probable economic results, administrative complexity and costs to society and with which a method of analysis is developed. Moreover, we believe our discussion will offer some information about the consequences of any measures aimed at substantially accelerating economic growth in the type of economy found in the United States. Although some chapters of the book deal primarily with the particular scheme on which we focus, others are concerned primarily with the general effects of the entire family of similar measures aimed at speeding up economic growth.

We do not claim that the growth scheme to which we pay particular attention is politically attractive. Indeed, in the nature of the case we expect that almost everyone will find it more or less objectionable. This point will be discussed in somewhat more detail in a brief chapter on the general problem encountered in any attempt at gaining political approval for major economic legislation. It can be foreseen, for example, that the scheme will be criticized for penalizing those whose interests are identified with industries' declining through no fault of their own, and for rewarding those who, possibly for reasons of luck rather than merit, are engaged in growth industries. Such objections are understandable. We wish to point out, however, that *any* growth scheme sufficiently powerful to produce a substantial change in the decision patterns of private enterprise would be subject to similar criticism, for any such scheme would produce similar irritants. When the reader objects to any one of this family of schemes, he must recognize that he is likely to find any method of appreciably accelerating output too costly.

6. Social overheads. There is one final limitation to our study to which we must draw attention. Our proposal is confined to the operation and performance of the private enterprise economy. However, acceleration of economic growth also demands accumulation of various productive assets which private enterprise finds impossible or unprofitable to provide at all, or which it finds impossible to provide in sufficient volume. These shortcomings therefore call for public expenditures of a growth-promoting type on education, research, public health, many kinds of public construction, and on improving opportunities for minorities, notably American Negroes, subject to impediments that keep them from contributing as much as they are capable to the country's production and the productivity of its labor force. In an economy which grows, and hence changes, more rapidly, there may also be special advantages, on grounds of efficiency as well as equity, in designing programs which help to rehabilitate workers with obsolete skills and local communities heavily engaged in declining industries.

A sufficiency of such expenditures is indispensable to accelerated economic growth and is complementary to the kind of growth scheme which forms the main subject of the present volume. We realize that proposals for such Government outlays are more easily made than appraised. They raise difficult problems concerning the desirable amount of such expenditures and their distribution over various specific investments in "social overhead." They also raise complex questions on methods for obtaining quality in education or research. In fact, available knowledge about these matters is deplorably small and should itself be increased as rapidly as possible. In this volume, however, our effort has not been applied in this direction.

But, although our contribution to the study of accelerated growth is thus very limited in scope, we feel no need to apologize for this limitation. If the United States becomes seriously interested in improving its economic growth performance, and hence in rapidly increasing the available knowledge of the conditions and consequences of accelerated growth, the appropriate research strategy at this stage seems to us to call for many individuals and groups to engage in many specific studies rather than in attempting to cover the subject in all its forbidding entirety.

· 3 ·

Proposals for Increasing the Growth of National Output

WILLIAM J. BAUMOL

The primary purpose of this chapter is to describe the rather radical proposal for increasing the rate of growth of national output which is used for illustrative purposes throughout this book. At least partly because they are so far out of line with the standard ideas on the subject, most readers will doubtless find these suggestions to be highly unpalatable. Yet it shall be argued presently that, given the growth objective which we are investigating, there is not very much choice among alternative means; any powerful and acceptable program to accelerate the nation's output flow is likely to have much in common with the machinery which is about to be described. The real difficulty in accepting such a course of action is that many of us are unhappy at the magnitude of the price in dislocation of existing arrangements which it is necessary to pay in order to achieve some very significant increase in growth.

1. General characteristics of the proposals. The class of proposals which are discussed in this volume involves two basic characteristics: first, their instrument consists in incentive payments to private enterprises which are designed to induce them to increase their contribution to economic expansion, and second, over-all fiscal methods are used to supply these inducements. It is our belief that almost any effective and acceptable method for stimulating growth will share these two characteristics or will employ very close substitutes for them.

The use of *over-all fiscal instruments* is necessitated by our desire to avoid direct governmental interference in the affairs of the individual or business firm, and detailed central planning and direction of various parts of the economy. An explicit set of subsidies might lead firms to increase their output just as effectively as a general change in the tax laws or other such impersonal fiscal measures. However, an industry-by-industry subsidy program will usually involve an unacceptable degree of central direction. This will be necessary because specific decisions on the distribution of the subsidy payments are required to determine who will receive them and in what amounts. Fiscal (or monetary) measures are the ideal instrument by which the relative attractiveness of different economic activities can be changed without explicit discrimination among industries, firms, and individuals.[1]

Similarly, we believe that *pecuniary inducements* are essential in such a proposal. To see why this is so let us briefly examine some of the alternatives. The number of broad possibilities is, in fact, rather small. What is needed in an effective growth program is a mechanism which channels economic

---

[1] This does not mean that such over-all fiscal measures are necessarily neutral in their effects on different industries. For example, in a low-income economy a reduction in taxes (particularly if it goes largely to poorer people) will probably increase the demand for food and clothing more than that for luxury goods.

The important feature of *over-all* fiscal instruments is that their operation does not require more or less arbitrary decision by government personnel, and they thus protect the public from the fallibility of the administrators' judgments and from the arbitrary exercise of their authority.

activity into expansionary directions, which leads people to work for increased productivity and to increase the proportion of their incomes devoted to investment. Three basic means for providing this sort of motivation or its results have been either adopted or at least considered elsewhere.

The first of these we may refer to as Education and Moral Suasion—attempts by means of exhortation and propaganda to get the private sector to save and invest more, to work harder, to reduce featherbedding and resistance to innovation. The effectiveness of such an approach is questionable, and, at best, its results are likely to be discouragingly slow. We can surely have little confidence in a growth policy which adopts moral suasion as its main instrument.

A second type of policy approach to the stimulation of growth involves the use of coercive measures to provide the motive for the cooperation of the public. What the government cannot achieve by voluntary public action, it may hope to accomplish by police methods. It can, for example, set up productive norms for management and labor and enforce them by means of severe penalties. There is some question as to the extent to which even the totalitarian countries have been relying on undisguised coercion. In any event, whether or not such methods have been effective elsewhere, they are totally incompatible with the idea of a free economy and must therefore be rejected by us out of hand.

A third class of growth policy involves primary reliance on direct government investment. What a government is unable to get its citizens to do, it may have to do itself. Investment can be increased by direct or indirect government expenditure for this purpose out of funds obtained by borrowing and taxation. Here is an approach which has been employed, and employed successfully by the totalitarian countries.

We cannot afford to reject this last instrument completely.

In some areas, the investment of public funds will have an indispensable role in any effective program for the stimulation of economic growth. In particular, there is need for federal aid to education and to stimulate the flow of new ideas and men who are trained to produce them. I believe that the long-run importance of this need can hardly be overstressed. Nevertheless, except in these and a few other specific and carefully selected fields, heavy reliance on governmental investment as a primary stimulus to economic expansion is clearly incompatible with our economic ideals. For it must progressively reduce the role of the private sector in relation to that of the government and is therefore inherently subversive of the system of private enterprise.

Having largely ruled out three possibilities: the government doing the job itself, forcing the public to do it, or getting private individuals to do it voluntarily, there remains only one alternative. We must make it worthwhile for the individual to bend his efforts in the desired direction. An appropriate system of rewards must be established, and, of course, financial rewards are the most easily administered and most generally accepted. This, then, is what we take to be the second feature of any promising growth stimulation proposal, a system of pecuniary incentive payments.

2. Outline of the proposal. The purpose of the plan to which we now turn is to tie the earnings of a private enterprise closely to its contribution to economic growth. It is proposed to do this by an extension of the standard industrial incentive compensation plans, the arrangements for "payment by results" which are designed to increase the productivity of employees by basing their remunerations at least partly on their outputs. Specifically, the illustrative proposal set forth here calls for a combined system of taxes and rebates which will be applied to almost all business firms.[2] Although the taxes could be levied on any appropriate basis, for example, along the lines of current business taxes (but above their present levels), we have developed the proposal on the assumption that these taxes would be based on value added. However, each firm would be eligible for an exemption or rebate from these taxes. The level of its exemption would depend upon the percentage growth of the firm's value added on *goods which it actually sells* compared with the firm's value added in the preceding year. The level of exemption would be proportional to the level of growth in value added.

This may be illustrated by a hypothetical example. If the 'target' rate of growth were set at 5 per cent and an additional tax of 1 per cent were levied on the value added by each firm, tax rebates could be scheduled so that firms just achieving the desired level of rate of growth would neither pay additional taxes nor receive any tax advantage. Thus the firm achieving the 5 per cent level would be taxed an additional 1 per cent and receive a 1 per cent rebate. In contrast, since the tax rebate would be proportional to rate of growth, the firm achieving a rate of growth greater than 5 per cent would receive a rebate larger than the additional tax, while a firm whose rate of growth fell below the target figure would receive a rebate smaller than the additional tax. In this way, growth would be rewarded and lack of growth penalized. The following schedule is purely hypothetical as far as the actual figures go but illustrates the way in which such a scheme would work.

As has already been indicated, one aim of the proposal is to avoid the use of detailed central direction of the economy. It seeks to give full scope to the ingenuity and enterprise of

---

[2] For a more detailed description, including a discussion of various appropriate exceptions, see the next chapter.

Per Cent of Increase in Value Added	Per Cent of Value Added as Additional Tax	Per Cent of Value Added as Rebate	Net Per Cent of Value Added as Tax (−) or Rebate (+)
0	1.0	0	−1.0
1	1.0	0.2	−0.8
2	1.0	0.4	−0.6
3	1.0	0.6	−0.4
4	1.0	0.8	−0.2
5	1.0	1.0	0
6	1.0	1.2	+0.2
7	1.0	1.4	+0.4
..	..	..	.....
20	1.0	4.0	+3.0

the private businessman. He would be able to decide on the areas into which he could expand most effectively. A firm in a static industry would thus be driven to invest in more dynamic sectors of the economy. Since rate of growth would be measured by the *value* of over-all company sales, sales of a new product could make just as much of a contribution as increased output of its current product line.

It is to be noted that a monetary measure of the growth of company sales and value added is required for two reasons:

(1) In the multi-product firm which composes the bulk of our industry, no single physical measure of company output is really possible.

(2) A value measure is required to permit and encourage industrial mobility in accord with the plan's growth objective (and because mobility is desirable for other well-known reasons). Clearly, firms will be encouraged to expand into other industrial fields only if they can be given tax rebate credit on these additions to their product line, something which can be accomplished conveniently with a common monetary measure of output.

Unfortunately, the use of a price measure leads to an

extremely unhappy complication which can be a source of all sorts of administrative difficulties. In order to reward real increases in value added and not an increase based merely on rising prices, the rate of growth would have to be measured in terms of the price of a product as of a certain date, that is, in terms of some fixed base period price. We are inclined to consider this one of the most serious difficulties involved in the proposal and have no desire to minimize the problems involved in the choice and administration of an appropriate set of base period prices.

Professor Edgar O. Edwards of Rice University has proposed a variant of the scheme which has just been described. He suggests that there would be advantages to a program which tied ". . . a tax rebate or subsidy . . . to the rate of growth of capital [rather] than to the rate of growth of value added. . . . If we were to tie a tax rebate or subsidy to the rate of growth in investment and couple this with inducements which would increase the supply of savings and the supply of labor, a more effective overall program should result." This at once raises the question whether value added or investment (or capital) is the better measure of achievement for a growth program or whether there exists some still more appropriate alternative, a subject which will be discussed later in this chapter.

3. Demand for the increased outputs. One critic has written that ". . . the most serious limitation to business expansion lies in the fact that the business managers' market expectations did not justify a more rapid increase in the capacities of their respective firms." This comment is preceded by the remark that ". . . in a free enterprise economy we assume that the profit motive (irrespective of how it is defined) leads businessmen to utilize opportunities for expanding their business undertakings. The opportunities consist primarily of anticipated markets."

If the implication is that an adequate growth program can be made up entirely of measures for keeping up the level of effective demand, we must strongly disagree. Even in periods with considerable backlogs of demand there was little evidence of really substantial rises in the rate of economic growth. Increases in demand which are permitted to run ahead of productive capacity are likely to result only in inflation. A growth program must include the means for bringing forth larger supplies as well as increases in demand.

However, while adequate demand is not a sufficient condition for a growth program it must certainly be considered a necessary part of any such plan. Increased output levels can only be maintained if markets can be found for them.

For this reason it is important to note that the proposed growth program involves no serious restriction on fiscal and monetary policies. It is compatible with standard fiscal and monetary measures which are designed to maintain a high level of employment and price stability. In fact, the tax and exemption levels can be varied independently so as to produce a budget surplus when there is danger of inflationary pressure and a deficit if there is serious unemployment.

Clearly it would be incumbent on the fiscal and monetary authorities to try to assure a demand for any increases in outputs which result from the program by means of some combination of the well-known measures available for stimulating effective demand. However, we would think it desirable that this be done in a very conservative manner. Perhaps it could be done by aiming to have demand just barely keep up with supply in order to hold a fairly tight rein on inflation and to keep producers on their toes, by making them fight for their markets and thereby maintaining pressures for reduced costs and increased productivity of their resources. Indeed, a really effective growth program will, at least at first, have more difficulty producing the necessary savings than in keeping up the level of effective demand. This difficulty will arise because increased growth is very likely to require a substantial spurt in investment, and during the interval which must elapse before it adds materially to output, the public must be induced to reduce its demand for resources in order to make the investments possible. This can either be achieved by an inflationary process which robs the consumer of his purchasing power, or, as is doubtless far more desirable, by means of fiscal measures designed to reduce consumption demand. In either case, however, there must be some reduction in the output of consumer goods and a corresponding increase in saving.

Thus, it must be emphasized, a growth program should not be misrepresented as a pure bonanza for the consumer. Although in the long run he would benefit as a result of the more effective pursuit of the national purpose which would be made possible for the government, as well as from any direct increases in consumer goods production, in the short run economic growth must mean very real sacrifices for the consumer. The recent history of the Soviet Union and the relatively short shrift it has given to its consumers should leave us very little doubt on this point.

4. Control over the composition of output. One of the most obvious objections to the entire plan is its lack of discrimination between various types of output. The production of mouth-organs, microscopes, and missiles may not all have equal value (per dollar of market price) from the point of view of "the national purpose" and yet the proposal offers them equal rewards.

It can be argued that an increase in just about any output

must bring with it some expansion in over-all productive *capacity* which may be what we need most urgently, and, moreover, that the attempt to keep up with the mercurial tastes of consumers will increase the flexibility of the productive system and leave it less subject to obsolescence than will the manufacture of carefully specified military equipment.

However, the real answer to the objection that the growth proposal does nothing about the composition of output lies in careful planning of the magnitude and nature of governmental expenditures. The major objective of the program, as has already been indicated in Chapter 1, is to provide the resources for military expenditures, for more research and education, for aid to underdeveloped areas, and the like. Suppose, for example, that the program were able to achieve a 5 per cent rate of growth. If consumer demand were to take up 2 of this 5 per cent, the government could increase its expenditure by the remainder (thus automatically providing the required demand for the increased output).[3] Moreover, we can be sure that private businessmen would then seek to produce the appropriate commodities. They only receive credit toward tax rebates for goods actually sold, and with the government, for some time at least, constituting the most important sector with growing demand, business would find it all the more necessary to provide the goods which the government is willing to purchase. So long as the public sector of the economy is careful in the formulation of its demands, then, we believe the composition of output can largely be left to take care of itself. Certainly on that portion of the increased production which

---

[3] Thus, for example, if we start from a position where 75 per cent of national output were going to the private sector and 25 per cent to the public sector, this would result in a rise in resources to 77 per cent (of original total output) to the private sector and to 28 per cent of previous total resources for the government. Then public outlay would be increased by 12 per cent (from 25 to 28) by this procedure!

does go to consumers, we believe purchasers should be permitted to continue to decide output composition for themselves on the basis of our current approximation to consumer (or, rather, public) sovereignty. We would be most reluctant to see someone in authority put in a position to decide what consumers' goods we ought to purchase for our own good!

5. Allocation of resources to non-growing industries. One frequent first reaction to our proposal is that it would tend to drive static industries out of existence even if it is socially desirable that they continue operation at, say, a constant level of output. We do not believe that this is a necessary consequence of the plan. To indicate the reasons for this assertion it is first necessary to discuss briefly the allocation of resources among different industries which might be expected to result from the plan.

The discussion need concern itself almost exclusively with the case of easy mobility of resources since it is probable that obstacles to movement must slow down the rate of resource allocation to "growth industries" and the rate of decline of industries whose outputs would have been static in the absence of the tax-rebate scheme.

Clearly, one would expect the proposed plan to lead some firms to leave industries with static markets and to enter the production of items whose demand is increasing most rapidly. The effect would be a reduction in number of firms in declining industries and an increase in the number of companies in expanding areas. This, by itself, can suffice to produce a dynamic equilibrium at least for a time because, if there is a reduction in the number of firms producing a commodity whose market is constant, each of the remaining companies can increase its sales by increasing its market share. To take an extreme illustration, assuming all of them to be identical, if half the firms leave such an industry, each of the remaining companies may be able to double its sales.

Similarly, the influx of new firms into growing industries will reduce concentration there, and the influx will thus cut down on the amount of expansion which can be achieved by any one firm. Thus the rate of transfer of capital will tend to limit itself and will achieve a moving equilibrium when firms can expect on an average to achieve the same rate of growth in all industries no matter whether an industry's market is growing rapidly or even contracting.

This state of affairs cannot continue indefinitely because, as it has been described up to this point, it must tend in the long run to involve a complete transfer of capital out of the static and the declining industries. However, this would be the whole story only if the firm's sole source of income were the tax rebate. It must not be forgotten that under the tax-rebate plan it still pays a firm to be profitable! That is, if the ordinary profits in an industry are sufficiently high, it will pay a firm to remain in that area of operation even though it offers little or no rebate opportunity through output expansion.

The upshot of the matter is this. If output growth is a sufficiently important objective, it is good economics to require that people be made to pay more for activities which hamper it. They will still be able to get the products of declining industries but only if they are willing to pay the price, enough to keep firms in business without a tax rebate. The allocation of resources could still be explained in terms of essentially the same marginal principles as apply today, but there would have been a change in the social priorities which would be reflected in higher prices of those products that serve as a drag on the expansion of output. Similarly, static industries which are needed to keep expanding industries in business would command higher relative prices for their products; the tax rebate of the growth industries would be passed on to them in the form of higher input prices which would be required to keep these growth supporting companies in business. It should be noted that this change in allocation of resources can be made either larger or smaller by an appropriate modification in the levels of taxes and rebates, by making them as large or modest in magnitude as is considered appropriate.

6. Alternative growth criteria. Professor Edwards' proposal (which was described toward the end of Section 2 of this chapter) makes it clear that output is not the only reasonable measure of the firm's contribution to economic growth. Several alternative indicators of growth readily come to mind: output per capita, output per man hour of labor (or per unit of some index of availability of resources), total output (GNP or NNP), and investment (or capital).

Where the primary aim of a program of economic expansion is an improvement of living standards it has sometimes been suggested that per capita output is the most appropriate index of achievement, and for this reason it is often accepted in the literature as the most reasonable criterion of accomplishment for the underdeveloped areas.

However, for our purposes, a total output growth criterion seems to be more appropriate than output per capita because our growth program is designed primarily as an instrument of military and diplomatic policy rather than one to increase levels of consumption. But for this purpose, per capita output is of rather limited relevance. Military strength depends in large part on the absolute size of a country's armed forces and its stock of equipment and not so much on the per capita resources of its inhabitants. Indeed, at least within limits, an increase in population can add to a nation's military and diplomatic power even though it results in a reduced output per head. For this reason per capita output is not a very satisfactory growth measure for our purposes.[4]

The other alternative criteria of growth achievement, the rate of investment (or the stock of capital) or output per unit of resources, have much more to be said for them. The stock of capital can be considered a measure of our productive *capacity*, and it may reasonably be argued that our international position will be helped more by an increase in capacity than by a direct increase in output. If a protracted "limited war" should arise, for example, we may ultimately be helped more by having the industrial equipment with which to produce military supplies, than by a high output level in the recent past, even if much of it consisted in military equipment (which so often suffers from rapid obsolescence).

Similarly, it can be maintained that output per unit of resources (per man-hour) is a measure of how effectively we have learned to use what we already possess and that this attribute is highly important for our adaptability to emergency situations.

Each of these points of view seems to have some considerable merit, and we attempt no categorical recommendation among them at this stage, especially since the basic proposal of this

---

[4] There are also other reasons for rejecting a per capita output growth criterion:

(1) It is for all practical purposes impossible to evaluate the effect of the behavior of the individual firm on the size of population and to establish a system of payments to the firm based on its contribution to output per capita as distinct from total output.

(2) In the United States, unlike some of the underdeveloped areas, population size is not a pressing economic problem. Moreover, we have no good grounds on which to predict the demographic effects of a growth program in this country, and it is not unreasonable to assume that the rate of population growth is an economically exogenous variable which is largely independent of the likely course of economic events. If this is an acceptable approximation to the facts, it follows that the program which is most effective in increasing total output will automatically make a near maximal contribution to output per capita (since, with the denominator fixed, we can maximize the value of the fraction total output/total population, by maximizing its numerator).

chapter is readily adaptable to any of these criteria. It is, however, pertinent to remark that each of them has its drawbacks as well as its virtues. For example, if tax rebates to firms were based exclusively on investment, it might induce companies to overstock on equipment since the combination of the tax advantage and the businessman's frequently sanguine expectations of the future could make it attractive to put in items for which there is no current use, equipment which would tie up resources in its production and maintenance and which would be subject to deterioration and obsolescence even though it went unused.

The appropriate choice among these criteria depends also on another element, the real administrative costs which they involve. If one criterion, A, were judged slightly more to the point than another, B, it might nevertheless be preferable to employ B if it permits a very considerable simplification of administrative problems. Primarily for this reason, I am inclined to reject an output per unit of resources criterion. The practical difficulties of finding an acceptable index of the level of resources and of making allowance for natural technological differences among industries in the quantity of resources required per unit of output would appear to be nearly insuperable.

It is on an extension of these grounds that Professor Edwards has recommended an investment rather than an output criterion. He writes:

> An important [advantage of an investment criterion] relates to the fact that the rate of growth of the firm may be enhanced at the expense of other firms. When one measures the rate of growth in terms of value added it becomes extremely difficult to distinguish that part of an increase in the value added of the firm that is also an increase in value added for the economy from that part that is achieved at the expense of other firms.[5] A

[5] Note, however, that our growth proposal should not constitute a stimulus to monopolization by merger. Under its provisions a firm would

subsidy to investment is much more easily administered so far as this difficulty is concerned. The physical characteristics of plant and equipment make it relatively easy to separate newly constructed facilities from those acquired from other firms.[6] In fact firms already divide increases in their fixed assets into these two categories when they report to the Securities and Exchange Commission. It is my own feeling that a tax rebate or subsidy . . . might better be tied to the rate of growth of capital than to the rate of growth of value added. While ideally value added is a preferable concept, its measurement in terms which are significant for the economy as a whole is so difficult that one is forced in either of two directions—one must accept a costly and probably ineffective administration for the program or one must . . . administer the program in terms of an individual firm definition of value added and struggle with all of the bad side effects that this entails.

7. Some alternative programs. The proposals which have been discussed are, of course, not the only ones which have appeared in the literature. Although, in fact, the number of concrete suggestions has been remarkably small, considerably less than the number of statements arguing that a substantial rise in our rate of growth is absolutely crucial, there have been several interesting proposals which should be mentioned, though they will be commented on only briefly and superficially.

Most of these have involved alternative incentives for expansionary activities. The suggestions which are most fre-

---

gain nothing through an expansion by merger. The combined firm would, it is true, acquire whatever sales expansion could be achieved by the two companies together. But since its tax exemption would be based on its *percentage* rate of growth, this increased growth would also be measured up against the combined sales of the two firms in the preceding year. However, see Chapter 7, Section 5 below.

[6] But we feel that this distinction is partly beside the point. After all, one firm may be able to invest because it has taken markets away from its competitors and has thereby made it economically impossible for the latter to invest. In that case the investment program of firm A is merely a substitute for the program of firm B and constitutes no net addition to the community's capital stock, which is precisely the same problem as that raised by Prof. Edwards relative to a value added criterion.

quently encountered include more liberal accelerated depreciation allowances, lower tax rates on high bracket incomes, and lower interest rates. We are in no position to rule out these or some other possible forms of pecuniary inducement. We would, however, comment that some of them are likely to raise serious questions of equity, and their potential effectiveness, even when carried to extremes, is not in all cases clear. For example, even if all real investments were permitted to be depreciated entirely in one year for tax purposes, it seems highly doubtful that the resulting increase in investment would be anywhere near sufficient to produce, say, the much talked of 5 per cent rate of growth. Similarly, a reduction in upper bracket taxes might somewhat encourage saving and risk taking and add some incentive for overtime work, but even if progression in tax rates were to be eliminated completely after some reasonably medium high level of income, we see no reason to expect spectacular effects on the growth of national output.

It is true that if rates of interest could be forced down to zero or even to negative levels, any physically productive level of investment could be made profitable. But the problems involved in considerable interest rate reductions are very serious, to say the least. These difficulties have been examined adequately in the literature on the Keynesian liquidity trap, and the discussion need not be repeated here.

Another idea which has received rather wide publicity is the view that there be a stop to the secular reduction in the length of the work week which seems to have been falling at an average rate of one-quarter of 1 per cent per year. It has even been suggested that at the current rate of increase in per man-hour productivity, such a measure would just about serve to bring us up to a 5 per cent rate of output growth. But this suggestion, as it is stated, can only be considered playing with numbers since no one seems to have indicated why this is a particularly expedient route for increasing output, nor have we come across any specification of the machinery whereby it could actually be put into operation (that is, how labor would be induced to forego shorter hours as per capita wages continue to rise, and how employment would be found for this increased labor supply).

We conclude, then, that the proposal which has been described in this chapter is by no means the only available course of action. All sorts of variants are possible, some of them rather less extreme and therefore, perhaps more palatable. Particularly there can be quite a bit of variation in the type of pecuniary incentive payment and the index of contribution to growth on which it is based. However, we do maintain that the plan which has been described is a prototype for which there seems to be no readily available substitute and that most of the alternatives which have been mentioned are of the same family. It is for this reason that most of the discussion of this volume applies with little or no modification to these other plans as well.

Let us end this chapter as it began, by admitting that the proposal which it contains is hardly likely to evoke widespread enthusiasm. Yet, it is in the nature of the case that this should be so. We have no grounds to expect revolutionary results from routine policy measures. If the need for increased growth is really urgent, we must be prepared to give careful consideration to policy measures which represent radical departures from traditional practice, policy measures whose soundness is prima facie suspect because they are not rooted in long tradition and are therefore largely untested by experience. Unwillingness to consider such ventures into the unknown may turn out to be complacency at its most dangerous.

· 4 ·

The Fiscal Structure
of the Proposal

WILLIAM D. CARMICHAEL

In the preceding chapter the outlines of an illustrative proposal for accelerating the rate of growth of our national output were presented. The major features of the proposal were two: a new tax on business firms, levied on their output (or value added), and an accompanying rebate or subsidy, the level of which would depend on the rate of growth (or percentage increase in value added) achieved by the firm. In this chapter we shall spell out in greater detail the intended coverage and fiscal structure of this proposal. In the course of the discussion many problems associated with the use of this novel fiscal instrument will come to light, some of which will be explored here and some in later chapters.

For most readers the range of problems indicated here will no doubt confirm their mounting suspicions that this proposal is a costly and cumbersome device for stimulating growth. Indeed, the practical problems connected with this or any other radical, large-scale method for accelerating our rate of output are numerous and complex. Only after such problems have been carefully explored, however, can the desirability of embarking on a major radical program for stimulating growth be assessed.

In this chapter, then, we attempt to give a more complete

picture of the nature of our proposal and of some of the difficulties which it involves. We do not attempt here to provide a detailed and thoroughgoing legislative proposal. What follows may be viewed, rather, as the principal ingredients of the mandate of those assigned the task of drafting a new statute.

1. Coverage of the proposal. In order for the scheme to achieve maximum effectiveness, its coverage should be extensive. It should apply to all firms without regard to their form of business organization, with certain limited and specified exceptions. To the degree that firms are exempted from the penalties and rewards of this proposal, its impact on the rate of economic growth will be weakened, and undesired distortions of the pattern of growth will be introduced. Since the proposal imposes a net tax or penalty on firms which fail to grow, and since it involves complex and costly methods of compliance, one must anticipate considerable resistance to it and numerous requests for special treatment and/or exemptions from its coverage. Such requests will be supported with several different lines of argument. Favorable consideration of such requests, however, must be contained within narrow and carefully defined limits if an all too familiar process of erosion is to be prevented from fatally weakening the scheme.

The exemption of very small firms from both the tax and the rebate or subsidy aspects of the proposal can be defended on several grounds. Exempting such firms would vastly reduce the costs of compliance and administrative burdens associated with the proposal while incurring only a small loss of impact in terms of the total level of output or value added in the economy. Such an exemption would also permit the individual, or family-scale enterprise, the growth of which is limited by the capacity for work of the persons involved, to remain unaffected and unpenalized by the scheme. Moreover, if firms with relatively low levels of output or value added are exempted, a large portion of agriculture will automatically be excluded from the coverage of the proposal. Granted the objectives and methods of our current farm policy, the exemption of firms primarily engaged in agricultural production will be required in order to prevent this proposal and our agricultural programs from working at cross purposes with one another.

The level of output, or value added, which should serve as the cutoff point for exemptions is open to debate. A single exemption level must be established for all lines of endeavor in order to minimize the complexities and instances of special consideration associated with this feature of the proposal. For the purposes of illustration, a cutoff point of $1,000,000 may be suggested. With such an exemption level, the scheme would be applicable primarily to major manufacturing industries but would include large firms in service and professional fields as well.

Firms beneath the cutoff point should be allowed the option of joining the scheme, subject to the provision that once having entered into it they would not be permitted to withdraw, at least until their payments into the scheme had matched the rebates received with appropriate allowance for interest over the period in which they had been net recipients of funds under the proposal. This provision is essential if small and growing firms are not to be discriminated against, vis-à-vis their larger competitors. In the absence of such a provision, the scheme would tend to result in new projects being undertaken only in firms with output levels higher than the cutoff point.

Several other candidates for exclusion from the scheme will doubtless be proposed and the merits of each case must be carefully examined. Requests for exemption of firms in declining industries or in situations in which market forces make it very difficult to achieve growth will be numerous but must be firmly rejected. The adverse effects of this scheme on firms which find it impossible to expand their output in conventional or new lines of endeavor must be viewed as an integral part of the mechanism by which the proposal will stimulate the transfer of resources into areas of greater growth potential and accelerate our over-all rate of economic output.

A special case for exemption from the scheme may be made for firms in certain publicly regulated industries in which companies are prevented by Government regulation from expanding their operations into new fields or from disinvesting in current lines of activity. Railroads, which are required to maintain certain contracting and unprofitable passenger operations, are a case in point. Most firms in regulated industries, such as those in the public utilities, transportation and communications fields, will experience relatively minor difficulties in growing as a consequence of their regulated positions and should be included within the growth proposal. However, grounds for exemption may exist in instances in which the failure to grow may be attributed primarily to the limitations imposed by Government regulation. The determination of whether or not exemptions are to be granted in such instances should be made by a tribunal especially constituted to deal with this and other quasi-judicial problems arising under the growth scheme.

2. *The base of the tax and rebate.* The merits of basing the financial incentives or rewards associated with this scheme on output, or value added, were set forth in the preceding chapter. Two alternatives to value added were considered and rejected. Output per unit of resources employed was found to be unacceptable because of the almost insuperable problems involved in finding appropriate indices of the level of resource utilization. The level of investment was at least tentatively rejected as a base for rebates because of the fact that investment and growth are not synonymous and because the use of such a criterion might encourage investment in idle capacity.

That there are also certain very difficult problems associated with the use of value added as a growth criterion cannot be ignored. With one minor exception, this concept is unfamiliar in United States fiscal practice, and its use would occasion both an unusual degree of opposition and substantial costs of compliance. The definition of "value added" for the purposes of this scheme must be carefully spelled out, and a choice between the gross and net concepts of "value added" must be made. As we shall argue in detail in Chapter 5, *gross* value added will be the more appropriate concept; that is, depreciation should be included in the measurement of value added by the firm.

Another set of problems of considerable magnitude arises from the fact that value added must be calculated, for the purposes of this scheme, in such a way as to eliminate the effects of price changes. As was pointed out in Chapter 3, if increases in value added resulting from higher prices were not excluded in calcualting the base for rebates and subsidies, firms would be rewarded simply for raising the prices of their products. It is *real* or *constant-dollar* value added which must be utilized as the base for rebates or subsidies. The complexities associated with this requirement will be examined in detail in the following chapter.

The penalty or tax component of the proposal should have a base identical with that employed in calculating the rebate or subsidy, that is, real gross value added. If the tax were based, instead, on corporate profits, a situation would arise in which a firm experiencing an increase in both value added and profits would fare less well under the combined tax and rebate scheme than would a similar firm with an identical increase in value added but no increase in profits. If unprofitable increases in output are not to be favored (and this seems a reasonable requirement), the tax must be based on value added, not on profits.

3. The rate structure. The aim of this proposal is to stimulate, through the mechanism of financial incentives, the growth of real output. With regard to other aspects of the structure and functioning of our national economy, it should be designed in such a way as to be neutral in its impact. If it is to meet this standard, a given increase in output should carry with it a certain reward irrespective of the industry, the size of the particular firm, or the particular time period in which it occurs. This requirement of neutrality vis-à-vis factors other than the growth of output imposes certain limitations on the tax and rebate structure to be employed.

A hypothetical and simplified illustration of the structure envisaged was presented in the preceding chapter. The tax would be a flat rate of value added (1 per cent in the example employed in that chapter), and the rate of rebates or subsidies would be proportional to the rate of growth or percentage increase in the value added that was realized, without upper limit or ceiling. The proportional relationship between the rate of growth and the percentage of value added which shall be allowed as a rebate or subsidy is essential if a given absolute increase in output is to be similarly rewarded when achieved by firms of different size.[1] Consider, for example, an increase in value added of $1,000,000 as it might be rewarded (under

---

[1] In the following illustration the increase in value added is calculated as a per cent of the current, rather than the past, year's value added.

the illustrative rate structure presented in the preceding chapter) when realized by three different firms:

	Value Added by Firm	Increase in Value Added as Per Cent of Current Output	Per Cent of Current Value Added as Rebate	Size of Rebate
Firm A				
Before Increase	$ 9,000,000			
After Increase	10,000,000	10	2.0	$200,000
Firm B				
Before Increase	$19,000,000			
After Increase	20,000,000	5	1.0	$200,000
Firm C				
Before Increase	$49,000,000			
After Increase	50,000,000	2	0.4	$200,000

Any departure from the proportional relationships between the rate of increase in output and the rates of rebate illustrated in this example would result in the proposal's being non-neutral with regard to firms of different size.

It must also be noted that there is a floor on the possible net penalty under this scheme that results from the flat rate nature of its tax component. That is, when the rate of growth falls so low that the rebate is zero, the maximum net penalty will have been incurred. This means that a small increase in output will not be rewarded at all if achieved by a firm whose rate of growth is well below this maximum penalty rate. As a consequence, there will be a tendency for new and expanding operations to be undertaken in firms which have already been experiencing a positive over-all rate of growth.

Concerning the specific rate structures which should be employed, only a few guidelines will be suggested here. If the proposal is to exercise no net inflationary or deflationary impact on the dollar volume of economic activity, the pattern of tax and rebate or subsidy rates must be designed so that the proposal will "break even," that is, that the taxes collected will match rebates and subsidies extended. In greater detail, the total value added of firms covered by the proposal times the flat rate of tax employed must equal the total *absolute* increase in value added to be rewarded under the scheme times the rate of rebate or subsidy expressed as a per cent of the absolute increase in value added realized. In the example referred to above, the rebate was 20 per cent of the *absolute* increase in value added (a $200,000 rebate for a $1,000,000 increase in value added).

Working with this illustrative rebate level (although a quite different one might be defended), the rates of tax as a per cent of the value added required, if the scheme is to break even under various hypothetical growth performances, can be determined according to the formula

$$T = GR$$

where T is the tax rate (applied at a flat rate to all firms), G is the current year's aggregate increase in value added (by all firms covered by the scheme) expressed as a per cent of current value added, and R is the rate of rebate or subsidy expressed as a per cent of the absolute increase in value added achieved (in this case 20 per cent). In this illustrative example, if the proposal were to operate in a self-liquidating fashion, the relationship between the tax rate and the current rate of growth G, as defined above, would be as follows:

Rate of Growth	Tax Rate
1 per cent	0.2 per cent
2	0.4
3	0.6
4	0.8
5	1.0
. .	. . .
10	2.0

For example, if the over-all rate of growth achieved by firms covered by the scheme were 5 per cent, a tax of 1 per cent of value added would be required for the scheme to break even.

The practical determination of the rate structures to be employed would be made with this relationship in view. In such a determination, one would also have to bear in mind that the rate of growth achieved will itself be determined in part by the particular rate structure introduced (about which relationship more will be said in the following chapter). Prevailing concepts of equity or "fair play," however vaguely defined, would also, of course, impose outside limits on the rate of taxation and corresponding rebate structure which might be employed.

4. Firms with fluctuating output. Another problem necessitating further refinement of the fiscal structure will arise in connection with the treatment of firms with markedly fluctuating levels of output. As outlined up to this point, our proposal would provide greater rewards, over a period of years, to a firm with an increasing but highly fluctuating level of output than to a similar firm in which the increase in level of output is more evenly distributed. The problem is illustrated in the following example, which employs the same rate pattern as is used above:

| | FIRM A | | FIRM B | |
Year	Value Added	Rebate	Value Added	Rebate
First	$ 9,000,000		$ 9,000,000	
Second	12,000,000	$ 600,000	18,000,000	$1,800,000
Third	16,000,000	800,000	10,000,000	
Fourth	20,000,000	800,000	20,000,000	2,000,000
Total	$57,000,000	$2,200,000	$57,000,000	$3,800,000

In this example both firms experience the same total output over the period in question, and for both firms a comparison of the first and last years of the period indicates an identical increase in the level of output. But firm B, the level of output of which has shown marked fluctuations, stands to gain considerably more rebates or subsidies than firm A, with the more regular increase in output. For coping with this problem (as well as with other difficulties to be mentioned below), one might suggest the introduction of an averaging scheme, in which both the rate of increase in output and the level of value added employed in calculating rebates would be determined according to some sort of moving average. A far simpler solution may be proposed, however, in the form of an added provision that, in calculating increases in value added, the current figure should be compared not with that of the immediately preceding year, but rather with the previous high (or the high figure recorded during a stated number of preceding years). In the example above, the application of this provision would result in a rebate for firm B of $400,000 in the fourth year, and a total rebate of $2,200,000, identical with that of firm A.

5. *Fluctuating levels of over-all economic activity.* In discussing the rate structures above, we examined the relationships between the tax rate, the rebate rate, and the rate of growth which must prevail if the proposal as a whole is to "break even" or be self-liquidating. As an important corollary of the proposition stated above, we may also note that a given rate structure will result in the scheme's breaking even only at a single rate of growth (G). A decrease in the rate of growth such as might be associated with a recession in the economy would result in an excess of revenues over outlays under the proposal, with the consequent exertion of deflationary pressures.

Similarly, an increase in the rate of growth above that associated with the break-even level for a given rate structure would occasion a deficit in the operations of the proposal and a corresponding augmentation of inflationary pressures. In short, if the rate structures remain unchanged, the scheme will exercise a net destabilizing influence on the level of economic activity. The nature of this problem, and the remedies which might be employed in coping with it, will be examined more fully in Chapter 6.

One possibly fruitful policy instrument in such a case will be afforded by the possibility of varying the tax rate employed. This is apparent from consideration of the table illustrating the relationship between tax rates and rates of growth for a break-even situation presented above. The introduction of an averaging scheme, referred to in another connection above, would also lessen but not entirely eliminate the destabilizing consequences of this proposal.

Going one step further, proponents of an aggressive countercyclical fiscal policy might advocate the adjustment of the tax rate under this scheme in such a way as to produce a substantial deficit during periods of recession and a surplus during periods of inflation. Such a practice would be subject to the many familiar pitfalls associated with all discretionary countercyclical fiscal measures, and would be rejected by some as lying beyond the limits imposed by our current degree of economic knowledge and by considerations of political and administrative feasibility. In the absence of adjustments of the tax or rebate structures over the course of the cycle, however, it must be admitted that the proposal would operate, to a degree, as an "automatic destabilizer."

6. Some additional problems. Three further sets of problems should be noted here: those which would arise in connection with the introduction of the scheme, those associated with the formation of new firms, and those resulting from the acquisition of assets of other firms (or loss of assets to other firms) through sale or merger.

For the initial phase of the operations of this program, provision would have to be made concerning the base level of the value added to be employed in determining the subsequent growth performance of the firm. It is clear that the level of activity in the immediately preceding year could not be taken as a base because of the possibility that affected firms would take steps to contract "artificially" the level of value added during that year in order to qualify for greater rewards under the scheme. The preceding year might also prove unsatisfactory as a base in instances in which the year was one of an abnormally depressed level of economic activity.

Two alternative base measures of the value added, familiar from our discussion of firms with fluctuating levels of output above, may be considered. On the one hand, it might be provided that the previous high level of output of the firm (in terms of real gross value added) serve as the base. On the other hand, one could advocate some kind of average of the levels of output over several preceding years. With either provision there might still be some incentive to curtail output in the year immediately preceding the introduction of the scheme (in order to prevent the establishment of a new "high" or to lower the base average), but such incentives would very possibly be more than offset by the profits to be derived from maintaining a high level of output during that year. In the event that a substantial degree of curtailment of output during the preceding year was deemed likely under both of these methods, further alternatives could be suggested in which the immediately preceding year's output would play no role in the calculation of the base.

Questions will also arise concerning the treatment to be afforded new firms under this scheme. At the outset, a distinction must be drawn between the new firm (in a legal sense)
which has acquired all or many of its assets from a previously
existing firm and the new firm which has started from scratch.
As we shall suggest below, it must be provided that any firm,
new or otherwise, which acquires assets from another firm will
accept simultaneously a certain "base level" of value added,
to be employed in calculating its future growth performance.
For the new firm utilizing the assets of a previous firm, then,
the base level of output would be determined through analysis
of the output levels of the firm from which the assets were acquired. For the new firm starting from scratch, all increases in
output above the cut-off level (a figure of $1,000,000 was sug-
gested, at least for illustrative purposes, earlier in this chapter) would be subject to rebates or subsidies under the operation of this scheme. Such treatment would be necessary if the
scheme is not to discriminate against new firms.

The problems associated with the scheme's treatment of
mergers and other types of exchanges of assets among firms
would be difficult and complex and can be considered here
only very briefly. It is clear that in the case of a merger or the
outright purchase of one firm by another, the base level of
value added of the new or acquiring firm would have to include the level of value added (and presumably the previous
high level) of the acquired firm. In the absence of such a requirement, the scheme would provide a strong incentive for
the concentration of firms in the form of the added rebates
to be derived by the acquiring firm.

In the case of partial acquisitions and sales of assets, the appropriate guideline is also clear, but the difficulties in applying
it would be very serious indeed. The base value added of the
acquiring firm, in such instances, should be increased by the

amount of the previous high level of value added attributable to the assets in question when in use by the divesting firm. An equivalent reduction should be made in the base value added of the divesting firm.

In all probability the application of this guideline, and of many of the other features of the proposal presented here, would give rise to numerous problems of interpretation and to a sizeable number of requests for special treatment. If it was not apparent at the outset, it is certainly clear by now that the fiscal and administrative structure of this proposal is of necessity extraordinarily complex. The practical operation of a scheme such as this would require, in all probability, the establishment of some form of commission or tribunal to which powers of interpretation and negotiation of settlements in special cases would be delegated. The political problems associated with this aspect of the proposal are among the several costs which must be considered in deciding whether or not to undertake a radical program to increase our rate of economic growth.

· 5 ·

Measurement
of the Effectiveness
of the Tax-Subsidy Plan[1]

RICHARD E. QUANDT

The proposal to accelerate growth, which was outlined in the preceding chapters, involves some radical departures from standard types of tax and subsidy. In contemplating such a scheme, one may naturally wish to know in advance how effective the suggested tax-subsidy plan might be and what kinds of incentives it will provide for entrepreneurs. The task of investigating the effectiveness of the proposal seems to fall into two parts: (1) an investigation of the problems of measuring the relevant economic quantities, and (2) an examination of possible theoretical and econometric models which can conceivably be employed. Neither of these tasks has a simple solution. The proposal involves so radical a departure from current methods of taxation or subsidization that information on the economic quantities necessary for implementing the plan, and for evaluating its effectiveness, is not currently collected and published. Nor are there any definitive theoretical treatments which discuss the possible consequences of such a plan.[2]

---

[1] I am indebted to Mr. Paul Demeny for computational assistance and numerous helpful suggestions.

[2] But cf. R. A. Musgrave, *The Theory of Public Finance* (New York: McGraw-Hill Book Company, Inc., 1959). Chapters 13-16 are relevant in this respect.

Much of the discussion in the subsequent pages is therefore bound to be of a somewhat speculative nature.

The main substantive section of the present chapter is devoted to an analysis of some of the conceptual and practical problems involved in measuring the rate of growth of real value added. The problem of measuring money value added in an industry consists of measuring the excess of the value of output over the value of materials purchased. The problem of calculating real value added involves the additional step of adjusting the dollar figures of output and materials purchased for price changes. At the present time such figures are not directly obtainable except for extremely broad categories such as durable goods, non-durable goods, services, and so on.[3] However, even if such figures were collected for industries on the basis of a more detailed classification, it would not suffice for the purpose at hand. The implementation of the growth scheme hinges on the availability of real value added figures for every individual firm affected by the scheme. Even without more refined analysis, it is clear that this is a task of staggering magnitude. It also follows from the data problem that, at the present time, no definitive statement can be made concerning the probable differential effect of the growth scheme on the various industries, and that the introduction of such a scheme could not be seriously considered without being willing to bear the costs of the necessary data collecting machinery.

Section 2 of Appendix B, which is an integral part of this discussion but somewhat more technical than the remainder of the book, deals with the theoretical consequences of the scheme for a single firm considered in isolation. It is assumed in Appendix B (and this is a very strong assumption) that price stability is maintained in product and input markets by mone-

---

[3] Department of Commerce, *U.S. Income and Output* (Washington, D.C.: Government Printing Office, 1958), pp. 118-119.

tary and fiscal policy if necessary. The conclusions made there are meaningful but somewhat limited by the nature of the single firm approach which is employed.

Section 3 of Appendix B suggests some empirical procedures that could be followed to determine firms' reactions to the scheme, and thus, indirectly, the tax and subsidy rates that would have to be set in order to accomplish specified growth objectives. For the reasons mentioned earlier, no actual results could emerge from this phase of the analysis unless the scheme were in operation and the appropriate data were available.

1. Definitions and measurement: the value-added concept. The proposal to accelerate the rate of growth can be summarized briefly. It involves a flat rate penalty tax applied to each firm's value added and a tax rebate (or subsidy), the rate of which is determined by the rate of growth of value added. The use of the value added concept stems from the desire to relate the proposal as much as possible to the growth of national income measured by some relevant standard.

As is well known, national income can be defined in several equivalent ways. On the one hand, it is the sum total of all income payments (payments for productive services) such as wages, salaries, rent, interest, and profit. (For the moment the distinction between the net and gross concepts is disregarded here.) On the other hand, it is the sum total of the values added by all firms, that is, the sum total of value of output minus cost of materials purchased.[4] The identity of these two measurements is strongly suggested by noticing that the part of the value of a firm's output which is not matched by payments to other firms for materials and services can be decomposed into the various factor payments such as wages, profits, and so on.

---

[4] A third alternative is to define national income as the sum of consumption, investment, government purchases of goods and services plus net foreign investment.

The value added of a firm is thus a measure of the national income originating in that firm. It is therefore immediately clear that success in stimulating the growth of the value added of every firm is equivalent to accelerating the growth of the national income.

One still has to distinguish between net and gross concepts. The difference between Gross National Product and National Income is made up of Capital Consumption Allowances (and Business Taxes as well, although they are neglected here). The largest part of Capital Consumption Allowances is Depreciation which is simply an allowance made for the wearing out of capital equipment. The aggregate depreciation figure is itself decomposable, at least in principle, into the depreciation figures of individual firms. For the individual firm, one can thus distinguish net value added which is the sum of its factor payments and gross value added which is factor payments plus depreciation.

Before proceeding any further, one must decide which of the two value-added concepts is relevant for the growth proposal under investigation. It will be argued that gross value added is the proper base for the tax and subsidy payments and that the rate of growth in gross value added is the proper determinant of the subsidy rate.

The argument rests on the fact that a proposal to accelerate growth should, in order to have long-run success, stimulate the growth of the capital stock. The particular proposal at hand must, therefore, not be inimical to net investment. If the subsidy rate increases (linearly) with the rate of growth of net value added, investment in new equipment may be retarded. Consider first the example of a business firm which intends to increase its physical output by a certain amount. Other things being equal, it may be able to accomplish this in two ways: by increasing the number of laborers hired and utilizing existing equipment more intensively, or by purchasing additional equipment (and perhaps increasing the labor force slightly). Since an increase in capacity is likely to increase the annual depreciation allowance, and since this allowance must be subtracted in order to obtain net value added, the rate of growth of net value added may well be greater in the case in which output is increased without an expansion of plant and equipment. Consider Tables 1A and 1B which represent two illustrative alter-

	TABLE 1A		TABLE 1B	
	Year 1	*Year 2*	*Year 1*	*Year 2*
Sales	100	120	100	120
Materials bought	70	80	70	80
Depreciation	10	10	10	12
Net value added	20	30	20	28
Gross value added	30	40	30	40
Rate of growth of net	.50		.40	
Rate of growth of gross	.33		.33	

natives. Sales and the cost of materials purchased is the same in the two tables. In Table 1A the depreciation allowance is the same in two successive years; in Table 1B it increases slightly. The rate of growth of net value added is lower in Table 1B. If these are the two options available to him, an entrepreneur receiving subsidy payments, the magnitude of which depends on the rate of growth of net value added, may well decide to postpone net investment (the option represented by Table 1A), whereas in the absence of the scheme he would have preferred the option represented by Table 1B if labor costs under this alternative were at least two units less than under 1A. Imagine, for example, that labor costs are 20 in case 1A, and 17 in case 1B. In the absence of the growth scheme, net profits are 10 and 11 respectively, and 1B would be preferred.

Viewed somewhat differently, one may imagine that a firm will decide upon a particular course of action by calculating its operating profit and the net tax-subsidy payments accruing to it and choosing the alternative which maximizes the sum of these two items. Even if net investment were desirable from the point of view of operating profit, the firm might nevertheless avoid net investment because, if rebate payments were based on the rate of growth of net value added, under case 1A the gain in rebate payments might more than compensate the firm for any loss of operating profit. Clearly, the reason for the discrepancy between the growth rates of net and gross value added is the fact that net value added does not contain as a component the entire capital costs of the firm. A second example is provided by the firm which wishes merely to replace existing equipment with better new equipment but without a net increase in capacity. Again, the net value-added calculation may provide an incentive not to purchase new equipment. If the subsidy rate is calculated on the basis of the rate of growth in gross value added, it will be convenient to have both the penalty tax rate and the subsidy rate apply to gross value added as the base.

2. Measurement of real value added. As is stated in other chapters, it would be a serious flaw in the current proposal if its operation rewarded spurious increases in the value added resulting from price increases. In fact, without effective provisions to avoid such a possibility, every firm would have the incentive to raise its price if it could thereby achieve an increment in its value added. For this reason, the rate of growth upon which the subsidy rate is based must be the rate of growth of *real gross value added.*

The problems of measuring real gross value added are serious and are treated at some length in Section 1 of Appendix B.

The difficulties in performing the calculations for real value added are considerable.

(1) The classification for which sales (shipments) and materials purchased and value added are available are not generally the same as the one for which wholesale price indices are available. The former, contained in the *Annual Survey of Manufactures,* is the standard industrial classification. The latter, obtained from the *Wholesale Price Indices* of the Bureau of Labor Statistics, is based on commodity groups. The two sets of classification agree in a limited number of cases only.

(2) Even greater difficulties are encountered in obtaining price indices of materials purchased. In principle, one might follow the standard index computation procedure and attempt to construct such price indices by examining the input structure of various industries. One might, for example, ascertain on the basis of input coefficients the proportions in which various industries purchase materials and compile a materials price index by weighting individual materials prices by the percentage of all materials accounted for by each particular item. Here again, the price and industry classifications do not generally agree.[5]

(3) Whether price indices are calculated on an industry basis or firm basis, the "market basket" problem is likely to be troublesome. Price indices are usually constructed by weighting the prices of commodities composing the index by their quantities in some base period. A price index thus shows how much the market basket of the base year costs in the current year relative to its value in the base year. If the commodity mix changes radically, the price index can no longer be depended upon to measure the change in the average price of

---

[5] See, for example, W. Duane Evans and M. Hoffenberg, "The Interindustry Relations Study for 1947," *Review of Economics and Statistics,* XXXIV (1952), pp. 97-142.

the new commodity group. This may be a serious problem in any event, but it is all the more serious when subsidy payments are made partly in order to change the commodity mix, and the magnitudes of these subsidies depend directly upon the behavior of a price index.

(4) The value added and price index calculations must be performed firm by firm rather than by industries. Even if there were no market basket problem of the type described in the preceding paragraph, it would be improper to deflate the sales of a particular firm by a price index for the entire industry. In general, a given firm will not produce all the commodities produced by the industry to which it belongs and will often produce some commodities classified as belonging to other industries. If, then, an industry price index were used to deflate the firm's sales, its real sales and its real value added could be influenced by price changes entirely exogenous to the firm. Such a procedure would create the incentive for each firm (which the proposal intends to avoid) to attempt to raise its tax rebate by increasing prices. If an increase in prices raised the current dollar value of sales, "real sales" for the firm would on this definition most likely increase as well, since the deflator, containing items not produced by the firm, would tend to increase less than proportionately. It also follows that the price indices based on data relating to individual firms would have to be readjusted periodically to take into account both radical changes in the market basket and changes in the character of a firm caused by mergers. It is unnecessary to belabor further the difficulties inherent in these tasks.

3. Some empirical findings. It has been implied in earlier chapters that it would be inconsistent with the spirit of the scheme to set target rates of growth which differ from one individual industry to another. If a single over-all growth rate is set as a target for the economy, it is quite unlikely that the

TABLE 2

Rate of growth of real sales in percentage terms

SIC Class	WPI Class	Name	1950	1951	1952	1953	1954	1955	1956
2213	0324	Woolen and worsted fabrics	15.0	2.2	2.6	−8.2	−34.4	15.2	.6
2825	0331	Synthetic fibers	19.4	1.5	1.3	7.6	−.5	17.8	−2.6
2351	0621	Paints and varnishes	18.1	4.9	−2.8	13.1	−6.2	9.1	−3.2
2823	0673	Plastic materials	32.9	9.4	−.1	16.7	−1.0	27.4	21.4
2824	0712	Synthetic rubber	31.5	52.8	4.1	−7.0	−19.1	42.3	12.7
2431	0820	Millwork plants	27.8	−3.1	−2.9	−.9	1.9	17.5	−3.4
2671	0953	Paperboard boxes	20.3	3.6	−3.8	13.5	−1.1	10.0	−.3
3429	1041	Hardware, n.e.c.	12.4	−6.1	−5.1	26.8	−6.0	23.0	−10.9
3561	1141	Pumps and compressors	.4	41.7	9.8	−.3	−4.9	4.4	−4.1
3614	1173	Motors and generators	10.5	15.9	15.9	3.6	−17.6	1.1	12.8
3615	1174	Transformers	2.7	16.8	9.6	9.9	−6.6	−3.2	8.8
3616	1175	Electric control apparatus	−.4	16.1	17.0	9.8	−13.4	−4.4	18.4
2511	1212	Wood house furniture except upholstered	34.5	−7.6	2.3	11.4	−13.7	12.6	1.3
2515	1214	Mattresses and bedsprings	19.3	1.1	−2.3	12.3	1.9	11.7	−2.7
3581	1242	Domestic laundry equipment	44.3	−1.1	3.5	19.5	−6.6	20.9	10.6
3471	1247	Lighting fixtures	14.3	−2.2	−.9	20.6	−15.8	16.2	−.6
3229	1262	Pressed and blown glass, n.e.c.	20.4	−6.8	−1.2	6.9	14.5	−.5	.8
3221	1263	Glass containers	15.3	11.5	.2	1.1	−1.4	7.8	3.9
3241	1322	Cement, hydraulic			3.8	−.8	4.6	6.9	4.2
3272	1350	Gypsum products	19.4	2.4	−4.7	10.2	10.4	16.9	−5.4
3292	1373	Asbestos products	22.5	20.0	−.8	7.6	−7.9	12.3	−2.3
2111	1410	Cigarettes	3.1	1.7	4.5	−1.1	−3.1	4.9	5.7
2085	1442	Distilled liquor, except brandy	13.8	−1.2	−19.2	19.7	−19.5	10.4	9.5
2082	1441	Beer and ale	1.4	−.9	3.3	7.5	−8.9	4.6	2.1
3871	1543	Watches and clocks	31.6	3.1	−1.3	11.3	−21.1	−1.9	−1.4

70

marginal growth produced by the program will be balanced in the sense that the various industries will each have their current growth rates augmented by the same factor. In fact, some industries will grow faster than before, and others may decline more rapidly than before. The effect that such a growth proposal has on the various industries is relevant for at least two reasons: (1) it will influence the composition of output; (2) it can be used as a guidepost in determining whether the particular suggested tax and subsidy rates are appropriate.

It would have been desirable, therefore, to calculate the rate of growth of real value added for as many firms as possible. This was not feasible for reasons discussed earlier in this chapter. The figures in Table 2 represent two significant departures from what was desired. First, they refer to industries rather than firms. Secondly, the rate of growth calculated is that of real sales rather than real value added. The latter departure implies either that we are relying on the implicit assumption that the rate of growth of real sales is the same as that of real value added or that we are implementing a somewhat different proposal, namely one designed to stimulate sales rather than value added. Because of these departures and other difficulties that will be elaborated, the figures in Table 2 cannot be considered as more than illustrative.

Table 2 shows rates of growth of real sales for a selection of industries. BLS indices of wholesale prices were used to deflate the value of shipments as given by the *Census of Manufactures*. The industries were chosen in such a manner that the definition of the industry and of the price index applied to it were as nearly identical as possible.[6] Thus, the sample of industries covered in Table 2 is not random and includes only

---

[6] In this connection I would like to acknowledge the help of the BLS in making available to me a cross classification of wholesale price indices and SIC categories.

industries for which the deflation process could meaningfully be accomplished.

The figures in Table 2 show relatively large fluctuations over time. The cyclical component is apparent when one contrasts 1950-51 with 1953-54. However, the fluctuations are not uniform. In synthetic rubber the annual rate of growth varies between a 52.8 per cent increase in 1951 and a 19.1 per cent decrease in 1954. For cigarettes, in contrast, the swing amounts to much less, being a 3.1 per cent decrease in 1954 and a 5.7 per cent increase in 1956. On the whole, the fluctuations appear large, and it is fairly plausible that the fluctuations in the rate of growth of real value added would also be significant. A growth proposal based upon annual rates of growth would result in large swings in subsidy payments, and even firms with good long-run growth potential would tend to be penalized in recession years. Since the objective of the plan is to reward long-run growth, it would therefore be desirable to compute rates of growth on a moving average basis. The length of the moving average is debatable, although a three-year moving average is not unreasonable in view of the fact that, given the postwar experience, such an average would usually not include more than one full recession.

One can infer from Table 2 that (1) variations in rates of growth of real sales are considerable from industry to industry, and the growth scheme may therefore have marked effects on the composition of output; (2) variations in rates of growth are considerable from year to year, and some averaging technique will be required; (3) rates of growth respond to the business cycle to some extent (see the numerous negative rates in 1953-54) but unevenly, thus probably leading to cyclical changes in the composition of output.

Table 2 is, of course, insufficient for judging either the general effectiveness of the growth proposal or its specific effect upon the composition of output. Although no amount of speculation can be a substitute for experience derived from the actual operation of the growth proposal, as a minimum, one would require some kind of estimate of what difference various rate schedules would make to the firms concerned. It would, in particular, be desirable to compare the magnitude of net penalty-tax-subsidy payments to the firm's operating profits. It would seem reasonable to hypothesize that firms' reactions to the plan would be most pronounced in cases where operating profits were small in comparison to tax-subsidy payments. It is also plausible that firms would be induced to undertake actions which reduced operating profits slightly, provided that these actions resulted in significant increases in subsidies. Thus firms might well begin to manufacture parts previously purchased from other firms in order to increase value added, even though they were not as efficient in producing the parts as the former supplier.

Unfortunately there are serious difficulties in performing the relevant profit calculations. A sectoral calculation of profit is possible for corporations[7] (although not on a sufficiently detailed basis) but the data in any given volume of the *Statistics of Income* are based on firms presenting tax returns within the given fiscal year (July to June) and thus actually overlap three calendar years. Needless to say, the problem of calculating real values becomes formidable.

In general, the problems of measurement are a serious handicap in attempting to evaluate the future effectiveness of a growth plan. Some of these difficulties would be eliminated when the plan was put into effect by virtue of the fact that its administration would involve the collection of the very data which would have to be used to test its effectiveness.

---

[7] U.S. Treasury Dept., Internal Revenue Service, *Statistics of Income* (Washington, D.C.: Government Printing Office).

· 6 ·

Implications
of Growth Incentives
for the Problems
of Inflation and Unemployment

WILLIAM G. BOWEN

No policy proposal can be judged solely on the basis of how well it accomplishes a single avowed objective; the over-all impact of the proposed measure on all of our main objectives is, of course, the criterion that must be used. Other parts of this volume have investigated the workings of the growth proposal in some detail and have suggested ways in which we can hope to evaluate its effectiveness in increasing the growth of national output. The purpose of this chapter is to consider the likely side effects of the growth proposal on two other important objectives of economic policy: high employment and price stability.

Instead of discussing employment and price stability separately, it is more convenient to consider the effects of the growth proposal on both of these objectives concurrently. Perhaps the most clear-cut way of covering this ground is by dealing first with the broad, aggregative aspects of the problem and then examining the significance of such institutional factors as trade unionism and corporation price policies.

1. Aggregative aspects. For the moment, let us allow ourselves the privilege of ignoring the special problems that arise as a consequence of the existence of "market power" (trade unions and large corporations) in our economy. Given this simplification, what broad, aggregative effects on the level of employment and price behavior can we expect from the growth proposal described in previous chapters?

Looking first at short-run problems, there is no question but that the initial implementation of the growth proposal could have some immediate effects on the level of aggregate demand and thus on employment and prices. Increasing the incentives for growth is likely to produce a sudden increase in the demand by firms for inputs of all kinds, and particularly for such growth-inducing inputs as research personnel and additional capital equipment. If markets were already tight, and assuming that it would take some time for increases in the supply of goods to occur, such increases in demand would result in upward pressure on the price level. A temporary period of significant inflation is by no means inevitable, however, since the traditional tools of monetary and fiscal policy could presumably be used to counteract increases in aggregate demand that threatened to be destabilizing. Difficult problems of forecasting and timing would be present, but these are certainly not new problems and must be faced whenever we attempt to make any use of counter-cyclical, monetary-fiscal policy. In short, the growth proposal does not appear to raise any short-run stabilization problems that are new in kind or beyond the pale of existing stabilization techniques.[1]

---

[1] The fact that initial implementation of the growth proposal will require (assuming that resources are already fully employed) either restrictive monetary-fiscal policies designed to prevent a net increase in aggregate demand or acceptance of some degree of inflation is a direct reflection of the need for an initial transfer of real resources away from current consumption uses and into growth-producing pursuits. Some combination of

Turning now to longer-run stabilization issues, there does not seem to be any inherent characteristic of the growth proposal that will bring about significantly higher levels of general unemployment. One of the crucial aspects of this growth proposal is that it rewards increases in real output and sales and not increases in capacity alone. Therefore, there is no a priori reason to expect the growth proposal to encourage business firms to create excess capacity that might in turn result in a substantial imbalance between the demand for labor and the number of people seeking work. Businesses are rewarded for being able to produce more only if they are able to sell more, and so the growth proposal itself does not encourage "over-production," excess capacity, and general unemployment.[2]

There is even some reason to think that, by putting an additional premium on increasing output and sales, the proposal may help to encourage firms to keep employment high. This "plus" factor must not, however, be exaggerated. There is certainly no reason to expect that the adoption of the proposal will eliminate the ever-present possibility that the demand for goods and services will fall short of the supply. The main point is simply that the growth proposal does not seem to have any features which make for the chronic occurrence of high unemployment.

Nor do the aggregative aspects of the growth proposal raise any particularly serious threat of secular inflation. It must be

---

monetary-fiscal policies would seem preferable to the inflation alternative as a way of bringing about this initial reallocation of resources for a number of reasons including equity, efficiency, and balance-of-payments considerations. The length of time that it will be necessary for us to sacrifice current consumption will, of course, depend directly on how successful the growth proposal is in raising total output.

[2] The growth proposal may, however, increase the amount of what has been termed "structural unemployment." This possibility is discussed later in the chapter.

emphasized that the growth scheme under discussion here does not rely on continued injections of additional demands for goods and services to spur increases in the national output. Such demand-oriented growth schemes are indeed likely to lead to inflation, particularly if pursued at times when labor markets are tight and when companies are operating at near-capacity levels. The proposal we are considering here, how-ever, *need* not involve any pronounced and permanent change in the balance between aggregate demand and aggregate sup-ply and so need not bring about any new upward pressure on prices from the demand side.

The reason for hedging the above sentence is that whether the growth proposal by itself leaves the level of aggregate demand unchanged, depends on the relationship between the tax side of the proposal and the rebate side. If the tax side of the proposal yields less revenue than the Government pays out in rebates, then its net effect is to increase the level of aggregate demand. Conversely, the level of aggregate demand will be decreased if the tax take exceeds the subsidy payments.

Although the tax and subsidy schedules incorporated into the proposal may be designed in the hope that the Govern-ment will "break even" from this aspect of its activities, we cannot be certain that this will in fact happen. The most obvious reason why the combined tax-subsidy scheme may not have a zero net effect on the level of aggregate demand is that the Government's expectations as to the effects of the proposal on real national output may not be fulfilled. If growth rates of participating firms turn out to be lower than anticipated (so that the percentage increase in the real value-added of the "average" firm is less than the rate of growth at which subsidy payments to the "average" firm just equal its tax bill), the Government will make money on the scheme; in contrast, if companies grow faster than expected, subsidies will exceed taxes and this aspect of the Government's operations will show a deficit.

Consequently, the combined tax-subsidy scheme could have a net expansionary effect on the economy and thus augment inflationary pressures, tend to raise the general level of employment, or both. However, if the Government overestimates how fast companies will grow, the scheme will have a net contractionary effect on the economy and thus exert downward pressure on prices, reduce the level of employment, or both.

Whether such unanticipated effects on the level of aggregate demand are "good" or "bad" depends, of course, on the situation in the economy at the time when the change occurs. In a recession, a net expansionary effect would be helpful; in a time of over-full employment, the same expansionary effect would be a handicap. The crucial question is: Are there any reasons to think that the net expansionary and contractionary effects are more likely to occur at the "wrong" times than at the "right" times?

To answer this question, it is necessary to distinguish between two types of "error" that may cause a proposal designed to "break even" actually to produce either a surplus or a deficit. First of all, the Government may simply make a bad guess as to the general potency of the scheme and may thus over- or underestimate the actual change in growth rates that will result from the adoption of the growth proposal. There is, however, no reason to expect this type of error to go in one direction or the other, and so mistakes of this sort are as likely to be stabilizing as destabilizing.

Unfortunately, the second type of error is not so neutral. A surplus or deficit may result not from a general misjudgment of the effectiveness of the proposal in promoting growth, but from the cyclical behavior of the economy itself. That is, the real output of firms depends not only on the strength of growth incentives but also on the strength of demand in the market place. If there is a general drop in aggregate demand (in a recession), the output of firms in general will be reduced, the actual growth rate in the "average" firm will be below the long-term or "normal" growth rate, and thus firms in general will pay more in taxes than they will receive in subsidies.

Hence, we are forced to conclude that in times of recession a tax-subsidy scheme with a fixed, unvarying rate schedule will make matters worse by generating a budget surplus and thus decrease the Government's contribution to the level of aggregate demand. In a parallel fashion, the proposal will accentuate inflationary pressures in "boom" times by tending to produce a deficit. In short, the growth proposal has the undesirable property of aggravating cyclical fluctuations in the economy.

The seriousness of this difficulty must not, however, be exaggerated. The pro-cyclical tendency of the scheme is, after all, due entirely to the rigidity of the rate structure, to the fact that tax and subsidy rates are the same in recessions as in booms. To meet this problem, the growth proposal could be modified to allow cyclically-timed adjustments in the tax and/or subsidy rates.

Recognition of the possibility of varying the tax and subsidy rates in accord with economic conditions opens up another issue: To what extent should manipulations of the tax-subsidy rates be used as a positive instrument of fiscal policy? Adjustments of the rate schedules could certainly be used not only to offset the destabilizing effects of the growth proposal itself, but also to combat recessions and inflations generally. In fact, this might serve as the more flexible fiscal policy instrument that politicians and economists alike have been advocating for some time. However, attempting to use the growth proposal both to promote growth and to stabilize the economy might make the proposal so complex as to be unsaleable and so cumbersome as to be unworkable. The limitations of current fiscal policy instruments probably ought to be attacked directly and should not be used as the excuse for cluttering up the growth proposal.

As an alternative approach, fiscal neutrality might be achieved by changing the pay-off aspect of the proposal to insure that the subsidy payments will always be exactly equal to the tax receipts. This could be done by determining the subsidy schedule after the actual output figures for a given period have been reported. The subsidy schedule would have to be set up so that the firm that experienced the "average" rate of growth for all firms during the given period would receive a subsidy just equal to his tax bill.

These possible modifications of the scheme suffer, however, from administrative difficulties. It might be wiser to preserve the simplicity of the rigid rate structure and combat the cyclical disturbances by means of traditional monetary-fiscal policies. After all, the growth proposal does not raise any radically new stabilization problems; recessions and inflations will occur with or without the growth scheme. Nor is the growth proposal likely to initiate recessions or inflations. What the proposal does do is accentuate to some unknown extent cyclical ups and downs that originate elsewhere in the economy. Perhaps the simplest way of meeting this problem is to try to reduce the frequency and severity of all cyclical disturbances by means of an aggressive use of fiscal-monetary policy, recognizing that the growth proposal makes this normally desirable objective even more desirable.

One final aggregative aspect of the growth proposal remains to be considered. It is generally recognized that the success of monetary-fiscal policies in curbing inflations and recessions depends to a considerable extent on the political status of these policies. And, it is certainly possible that an added reward for growth might increase the political opposition to various anti-inflationary measures such as tight money and high taxes. For instance, if various members of the community are asked to pay taxes to subsidize economic growth, they may well be strongly disposed to demand that the Federal Reserve also make its maximum contribution to that same end by keeping interest rates low. Similarly, the adoption of a new tax (even though accompanied by a new subsidy) might be expected to produce renewed cries for lower corporation, personal, and excise taxes. Via this indirect political route, the growth proposal might aggravate the alleged inflationary bias of our economy.

2. Institutional aspects. So long as we ignore the existence of "market power" and other institutional imperfections (such as lack of mobility), it is possible to analyze the side effects of the growth proposal on employment and price behavior largely in terms of aggregate demand and aggregate supply. However, when we admit that strong unions and industrial concentration do play a significant role in the economy, things become considerably more complex.

The general significance of "market power" is that it forces us to recognize that inflation and unemployment can co-exist. Rather than considering unemployment and inflation as separate problems, it becomes necessary to study the relationship between these two problems, and, in particular, to try to determine how fast prices are likely to rise at alternative levels of unemployment.[3]

In the specific context of the growth policy discussion, the

---

[3] As a partial concession to prevailing linguistic habits, it may be noted that we are now discussing at least a part of what is often called the "cost inflation" problem. However, the phrase "cost inflation" is subject to so many interpretations and misinterpretations that it is best to avoid this terminology altogether.

relevant question now before us is: Would the adoption of
the growth proposal make matters worse by causing prices to
rise faster at given levels of unemployment? In discussing this
question, it is convenient to begin by considering the likely
effects of the growth proposal on the wage and price behavior
of individual firms that are within the "market power" sector
of the economy (that is, firms that are either strongly union-
ized, sell in a product market that is relatively highly concentrated, or both). The interaction between happenings in
individual firms will be considered subsequently.

The need for a price deflator. The first, and perhaps
most important, point to be made here is that without an
adequate means of correcting for price changes (and thus
making sure that only "real" increments to value-added are
rewarded) the tax-subsidy scheme would undoubtedly cause
wages and prices to go up more rapidly at given levels of
unemployment. In the absence of any price deflators what-
soever, firms that "administer" prices would have an obvious
incentive to raise prices since higher prices would, in all probability, increase the value-added (measured in current dollars)
of the firm. Similarly, firms would have less incentive to resist
wage demands of unions, since at least a part of larger wage
adjustments would be reflected in a larger value-added figure
and thus would bring a larger subsidy from the Government.

To prevent the growth proposal from encouraging purely
monetary increases in value-added, some kind of price deflator
is clearly needed. Furthermore, the use of any kind of economy-
wide, or even industry-wide, price index will not do since
individual firms could still make money by raising their own
prices. From the standpoint of the individual firm, an increase
in the price of its own products may be expected to increase
its own value-added (measured in current dollars) significantly,

but to have a much smaller effect on any industry-wide or economy-wide price index used to deflate monetary changes in value-added.

The only apparent solution to this problem is the use of price weights based on the prices charged in some base period by each individual firm. If such a specific price deflator could be constructed for each firm participating in the growth program, purely monetary increases in value-added would not be rewarded by larger subsidies. An acceptably equitable base date for all firms to use in tax returns may not exist; if this is the case, the growth proposal will encourage higher wages and higher prices, and the extent of this encouragement will depend directly on how broad an index it is necessary to use.

The growth proposal and union bargaining power. Even if we assume that an ideal set of price deflators has been found, the growth proposal may still lead to somewhat larger wage increases than would occur in the absence of the proposal. The reason is that any program rewarding high output will increase the bargaining power of trade unions by making strikes more costly to firms. A firm faced with the threat of a work stoppage would, if the growth proposal were in operation, have to contemplate not only the lower profits and possible loss of customer allegiance that a strike always entails but also the effect of the strike on the output of the firm and thus on the amount of subsidy it can expect to receive from the Government. Consequently, firms would have an additional incentive to avoid strikes by settling on the union's terms.

The quantitative importance of this increase in union bargaining power is very hard to estimate. In some industries work stoppages do not result in much of a permanent loss of output but instead affect mainly the timing of production.

Where this is the situation, the tax-subsidy scheme would not have as great an impact on union bargaining power.

An even more important consideration serving to minimize the tendency of the growth proposal to encourage industrial "peace at any price" is the floor under the penalty aspect of the proposal itself. It is very important to recall that under the proposal described earlier a firm that suffers an absolute decline in its value-added is hit no harder by the tax-subsidy scheme than a firm of the same size that simply stands still and records a zero increase in value-added. Both firms pay the same tax (assuming they have the same value-added in the base period) and neither receives any subsidy. Consequently, if a firm is having a bad year anyway and is not likely to record an increase in value-added in any case, the possibility of a strike will not pose additional financial threats to the company from the standpoint of the growth proposal.

In fact, under certain conditions the growth proposal may even encourage firms to take lengthy and severe strikes. The growth scheme not only may fail to raise the immediate costs of a strike, but also it may actually reduce the long-run costs of a serious strike as well. The explanation for this cost-reducing possibility is that the amount of tax the company will pay in the next period (after the strike) will depend on the size of its value-added, and a strike is very likely to lower value-added and thus cut the future tax liability of the company. In addition, the lower value-added provides a more advantageous base from which to raise value-added in the future and thus may result not only in lower taxes but also in higher subsidies.

Unfortunately, there is no way in which these speculations about the effect of the growth proposal on union bargaining power and wage behavior can be put to a satisfactory empirical test. If, however, experience were to indicate a need to lessen the upward pressure on wages (and thus on prices) emanating from this source, there are several ways in which this might be done. To illustrate, employers might be given more incentive to resist wage demands by providing that wage adjustments in excess of a certain amount must be deducted in computing the value-added of a firm. However, because of the difficulties in drawing up and administering a specific proposal that would be effective without at the same time being inequitable, it would seem best to postpone serious consideration of plans of this type until the need for such measures is more apparent than it is at present.

Productivity improvements and labor costs. We come now to a more encouraging aspect of the analysis. There is at least one respect in which adoption of the growth proposal might reduce, rather than increase, the magnitude of price increases associated with a given amount of unemployment. This possibility stems from the fact that the behavior of labor costs depends both on the size of wage adjustments and on changes in what is loosely called "productivity." The growth scheme would reduce upward pressure on labor costs to the extent that productivity improvements induced by the scheme are not fully offset by additional upward wage adjustments.

Some advocates of a more rapid rate of growth have gone so far as to suggest that one of the most important ancillary benefits of rapid growth is to be found right here; if the over-all size of the national output can be made to increase more rapidly, it should be possible to accommodate the wage demands of unions and the profit demands of owners without resorting to price increases. This estimate of the anti-inflationary benefits of growth seems a bit over-optimistic, however, for two main reasons.

First of all, producing more and producing at a lower cost

per unit are not necessarily synonymous. It is important to emphasize that the growth proposal under discussion here rewards increases in total output, not increases in output per man-hour or increases in output per unit of capital. Firms may well raise their output by discovering ingenious new ways of getting extra units of output from the same, or even fewer, units of input. However, output may go up in other ways as well. For example, the output of the economy could no doubt be increased substantially if all of us worked twice as many hours per week. Yet this type of increase in output is more likely to result in higher labor costs per unit of output (as efficiency falls off with increased hours of work) than in lower per unit labor costs. Furthermore, even if the avenues to larger output do entail lower labor costs per unit of output, this is no guarantee that total costs per unit will decline proportionately. Many techniques for raising output might well require additional capital per unit of output at the same time that hours of labor were being saved. The general point is simply that increases in total output may well be larger than the accompanying reductions in the amount of labor and capital needed per unit of output.

In the second place, it is unwise to assume that the behavior of money wages is unaffected by whatever gains in productivity do accompany increases in output. Increases in output per man-hour may themselves lead to increases in wages, and to the extent this occurs the deflationary impact of more rapid growth is dampened.

Where workers are paid on a piece-rate basis, minor improvements in the techniques of production are likely to be directly reflected in higher wages. In cases where time rates of pay are employed, productivity improvements may lead to higher wages by indirect channels; for example, by improving the profitability of the firm and thus increasing the appetites of the workers while at the same time reducing the inclination of management to resist wage increases. The general attitude of the workers and the political situation within the union movement are likely to be important determinants of the extent to which productivity improvements are offset by additional wage increases. Much depends on the determination of union leaders to receive a certain *share* of the total pie as opposed to their determination to obtain larger benefits for their own membership regardless of how well other sectors of the economy happen to be faring.

Wage-price problems resulting from changes in the composition of output and employment. If the growth proposal were adopted, it seems likely that the economy would be subject to more rapid changes in the composition of output than would occur in the absence of any such effort to increase the growth of national output. Although all firms in all industries would have the same incentive to grow, growth opportunities are not likely to be evenly distributed. If the opportunity to grow is, in some industries, limited by factors other than merely lack of initiative or incentive (for example, if it is hampered by a steady decline in the demand for the produce of the industry), then the penalty aspect of the growth scheme is likely to hasten the decline of such industries. Conversely, industries with unusually favorable growth opportunities would have their expansion hastened by the growth proposal. Thus, the normal ups and downs in the fortunes of different industries would be accentuated if the growth proposal were put into operation.

Because of various rigidities and "imperfections" in the economy, this speeding up of changes in the composition of output might well cause the general level of wages and prices to rise more rapidly at given levels of unemployment. It is generally thought that there is an important asymmetry between the effects of increases in demand and decreases in demand. Increases in output are likely to be accompanied by an increase in the rate at which wages and prices rise, whereas decreases in output are not so likely to be accompanied by decreases in wages and prices.

In short, wages and prices seem to be more flexible in the upward direction than in the downward direction, and, as a result, the more pronounced the inter-industry shifts in demand the more rapidly will the general level of wages and prices rise. This problem is complicated still further by the tendency of wages in the less fortunate industries to emulate the pattern of wage behavior in the more prosperous sector. Although a perfectly rigid pattern of wage leadership does not exist, large wage increases granted by the expanding and relatively high-profit firms are usually transmitted to some extent to other workers.

The probable magnitude of this side effect is, however, reduced by the definite possibility that the industries that would benefit most from the growth proposal would be those in which, for various reasons, production worker employment is declining. It seems plausible to assume that an extra incentive for increased output would have more effect on output and employment in the manufacturing sector than elsewhere. Furthermore it is production worker employment in manufacturing that has been falling behind employment trends elsewhere in the economy. In contrast, the sector in which employment has been growing most rapidly is the service sector (partly as a consequence of an increased demand for services as our incomes rise), and the growth scheme would not, in all probability, have such a pronounced effect here. Consequently, given these broad differential trends in industry employment, the changes in the composition of output induced by the growth proposal might not lead to as much of a *net* change in the composition of employment as we might normally expect.

Marked shifts in employment opportunities within different occupational categories are also likely to result from the growth proposal, and these inter-occupational shifts might be even more important from a stabilization standpoint than the inter-industry changes in output. Specifically, putting an added premium on growth would certainly lend further encouragement to the sharp increase in the demand for highly educated and highly trained personnel that is already underway. The present tendency for "white-collar" workers to comprise an ever-larger proportion of the work force would no doubt be given an extra push by the adoption of almost any growth-stimulating policy. The increase in the relative quantitative importance of white-collar workers as opposed to production and non-supervisory workers is likely to increase the general level of wages and salaries for some of the same reasons as a sharp shift in the composition of industry output. Wages and salaries of occupations in short supply will continue to rise at a relatively rapid rate while production workers will resist reductions in their relative pay scales.

There is one last implication of changes in the composition of output and employment that must be mentioned. As a result of the comparative immobility of the labor force (between areas, occupations, and, to a lesser extent, industries), more rapid shifts in employment opportunities are quite likely to bring about additional pockets of what has been called "structural unemployment." Employees located in the less favorably situated occupations and industries will have a difficult time readjusting. At the same time, shortages of labor in other areas, occupations, and industries are likely to produce bottlenecks.

It is, of course, hard to combat this kind of structural unemployment by means of general monetary-fiscal policies.

Mild, short-run doses of increased aggregate demand are not going to have much effect on employment in depressed occupations and areas; sharp increases in aggregate demand are likely to create severe inflationary pressures in other sectors of the economy and even then may not re-employ all of the dislocated workers. Perhaps a more promising approach to this particular problem is to allocate a portion of the increased output which it is hoped the growth scheme will generate to the retraining and relocation of the chronically unemployed.

7. General conclusions. The main points that have emerged from this general discussion can be summarized in outline fashion as follows:

(A) The growth proposal does not seem to raise any radically new threats to high employment and price stability; nor does it threaten to initiate cyclical fluctuations in the economy.

(B) Adoption of the growth proposal is, however, apt to aggravate our current stabilization problems in six respects:

(1) If the same tax and subsidy schedules are used regardless of economic conditions, the growth proposal would accentuate cyclical swings in the economy that received their initial impetus elsewhere.

(2) Rewarding growth might lessen the political appeal of anti-inflation policies.

(3) If it is impossible to administer a price deflator based on prices charged by each individual firm, the growth proposal will encourage firms to raise wages and prices.

(4) The bargaining power of unions may be increased by making strikes more costly to employers.

(5) Sharper changes in the composition of output and employment may cause wages and prices to rise more rapidly at given levels of unemployment.

(6) Additional amounts of "structural" unemployment may be created.

(C) In contrast, the growth proposal might lessen stabilization problems by:

(1) Raising productivity and thus exerting some downward pressure on labor costs.

(2) Providing a new instrument (the tax and subsidy schedule) that could permit a more flexible fiscal policy. (However, it is not clear that tax and subsidy rates designed to encourage growth should be used for stabilization purposes as well.)

It is important to emphasize that most of these stabilization implications are by no means unique to the particular growth proposal elaborated in this volume, but are, in some closely related form, involved in almost any policy aimed at increasing the national output.

It is also worth emphasizing that the proposal's undesirable effects on stabilization are not totally intractable. Some of its aggravating effects on stabilization problems (particularly B1) can be minimized by careful use of the traditional tools of monetary-fiscal policy. In other cases, modifications of the growth proposal itself could help if they were needed.

Unfortunately, precise, quantitative estimates of the effects of the growth proposal on employment and prices are simply not possible. All of the side effects do not go in the same direction, and the magnitude of the various side effects depends on many imponderables. The very "fuzziness" of the final picture does, however, warn against doctrinaire interpretations. Although the possible significance of undesirable side effects most certainly ought not to be minimized, it would also seem unwise, at this stage, to reject the growth proposal solely on the basis of its probable impact on employment and price stability.

· 7 ·

Growth Incentives
and Antitrust Policy

JESSE MARKHAM

The essential feature of the proposal to stimulate economic growth set forth in this volume is that it holds out to individual business firms a financial incentive to grow at a faster rate than the one traditional incentives can be expected to generate. It is assumed, then, that the proposed growth scheme will motivate firms to grow at a substantially higher rate than they would under existing incentives. Expressed differently, it will overcome some of the existing constraints on firm growth.

Because the proposed scheme rewards all internal growth which can be measured in terms of changes in real value added,[1] irrespective of the side effects of such growth or the means by which it is attained, conflicts may arise, as we have pointed out repeatedly, between the scheme and other public policies affecting firm growth. Conflicting ends among public policies call either for compromise or revision in the policies themselves. This chapter seeks to identify the possible areas of conflict between the proposed growth bonus scheme and antitrust policy, and the specific revisions of the latter which would have to be made in order to accommodate the growth proposal were it to become a new, urgent, and effective public policy.

---

[1] Small firms having value added of less than $1 million are possible exceptions.

1. *Antitrust policy and firm growth*. A serious assessment of antitrust policy, for whatever purpose, necessarily begins with the caveat that the antitrust laws and their judicial interpretation undergo constant change. In language similar to the Supreme Court's early dictum on the reasonableness of a given price, ". . . the antitrust policy of today may not be the antitrust policy of tomorrow." [2] Congress often amends the basic laws in the light of new economic problems and policies. The Robinson-Patman Act of 1936, the Miller-Tydings Act of 1937, and the 1953 McGuire Amendment to the Federal Trade Commission Act, all were ostensibly designed to arrest the decline of "small business"; the Anti-Merger Act of 1950 was aimed at curbing the growth of "big business." And even when Congress does not act to amend them, the courts often reinterpret existing antitrust statutes to accommodate new policies; they virtually suspended the antitrust laws in the period of the N.I.R.A.; and since the first Agricultural Adjustment Act (1933) and the National Labor Relations Act (1935) they have greatly limited the applicability of the antitrust laws to agricultural and labor organizations. There is, then, a degree of conscious and automatic adaptation of antitrust law to new policies, and there is no reason to assume that this adaptive process could not in part accommodate the proposed growth scheme.

Nevertheless, there are certain established antitrust policy principles that clearly conflict with a plan designed to stimulate economic growth through a system of bonuses geared to the business firm. Although most analysts of antitrust policy would undoubtedly agree that in the broad sweep of its history since 1890 antitrust policy has stimulated growth of the economy as a whole, they would surely agree also that antitrust policy as presently administered restricts certain forms of

---

[2] *Cf. Addyston Pipe and Steel Co.* v. *U.S.*, 175 *U.S.* 211 (1899).

growth of firms and prohibits certain practices firms employ which result either in their growth or the growth of other firms with which they carry on business transactions.

Fundamentally, the source of conflict between what anti-trust policy on the one hand prohibits and the proposed growth scheme encourages on the other, lies in the differences in the dimensions of the economic units toward which the two policies are applicable. Antitrust policy applies to the business firm in the context of the effect of its actions on a particular market; the growth scheme applies directly and exclusively to the firm. The former places a constraint on firm growth, whether its incentive be monopoly profit or a growth bonus, if it has market effects which the specific laws proscribe; the latter encourages and rewards firm growth, irrespective of how it affects particular markets. Accordingly, firms seeking success-fully to earn growth rewards may in certain circumstances do so at the risk of paying criminal and civil penalties for violat-ing the antitrust laws. In such cases the prospects of penalties will weaken the incentive the bonus provides, and the prospec-tive bonus will induce firms to take on greater risks of law violation. In short, the growth scheme and antitrust policy con-front the firm with conflicting incentives and controls.

2. *The Sherman Act and firm growth.* The antitrust provi-sion potentially in greatest conflict with the proposed growth bonus scheme is Section 2 of the Sherman Act, which makes *every* monopoly or attempt to monopolize a misdemeanor.[3]

---

[3] Section I outlaws contracts, conspiracies, and combinations, whether in the form of trusts or otherwise, which restrain trade. It has been primarily applied to agreements among competitors to fix prices, rates of output, or various terms of trade. Since such agreements are generally considered to *restrain* the growth of the participating firms there is no apparent conflict between this Section of the Sherman Act and the proposed growth scheme. On the contrary, it may be persuasively argued that they reënforce each other. See *infra.*

The annals of American business reveal striking cases where the process of monopolizing has been accompanied by staggering rates of firm growth. The early Standard Oil combine grew from a small per cent to about 80 per cent of refined petroleum sales in the short space of nine years; the early American Tobacco Company chalked up an equally impressive growth record. International Harvester, DuPont, General Motors, United Shoe Machinery, the Aluminum Company of America, R. J. Reynolds Tobacco Company, General Electric, and a host of other large American corporations have all grown at impressive rates, but in the process they, along with Standard Oil and American Tobacco, often found themselves defendants in antitrust cases. However, they also would have received handsome growth bonuses, in most cases even if growth by merger were eliminated, had the proposed growth bonus scheme been in effect.

To be sure, findings of fact in antitrust litigations reveal that in many of these cases the primary motive was monopoly reward rather than simple profit-induced growth. In some, however, it is not at all clear whether the monopoly incentive resulted in growth or the growth incentive incidentally, or unavoidably, resulted in monopoly power.

3. The Aluminum Company decision. Uncertainty as to which incentive may have governed is most clearly brought out in the case of Alcoa. After 1912 Alcoa operated under a consent decree[4] which denied it the usual means of attaining monopoly power. Under terms of the decree Alcoa agreed (1) to end arrangements for dividing international markets; (2) to terminate contracts with certain chemical firms from which

---

[4] *U.S.* v. *Aluminum Company of America,* Eq. 159 (w.d.Pa. 1912), decree in U.S. Dept. of Justice, Decrees and Judgments in *Federal Antitrust Cases* (1918), pp. 341-50.

it had purchased bauxite deposits, whereby they bound themselves not to enter aluminum manufacture; (3) to enter no
such contracts in the future, nor any which would prevent
others from obtaining bauxite, alumina, or aluminum, or
would control their price, nor engage in any mergers for the
purpose or with the effect of controlling output or price; and
(4) not to discriminate in price or service against any com-
peting fabricator in favor of a unit of Alcoa's own business.

Denied these means, Alcoa apparently relied on vigorous
and aggressive growth for financial success. It anticipated demand by doubling and redoubling capacity; it competed vigorously for other metal markets, and bought promising bauxite
deposits in anticipation of demand increases. In the three
decades following 1910 Alcoa increased its annual virgin aluminum production (and sales) by 2,500 per cent, reduced prices
from several dollars to fifteen cents per pound and kept profits
for most years below 10 per cent. It may well be that Alcoa
was motivated also by prospective monopoly reward, but most
of its policies were consistent with the motive of financial
success through vigorous growth. Judge Learned Hand, in his
famous landmark decision of 1945,[5] disposed of the issue of
Alcoa's motive by inferring the objective of monopoly from
the possession of substantial market power:

> The only question is whether [the *Alcoa* case] falls within the
> exception established in favor of those who do not seek, but
> cannot avoid, the control of a market. . . . It was not inevitable
> that [*Alcoa*] should always anticipate increases in the demand
> for ingot and be prepared to supply them. Nothing compelled it
> to keep doubling and redoubling capacity before others entered
> the field. It insists that it never excluded competitors; but we
> can think of no more effective exclusion than progressively to
> embrace each new opportunity as it opened, and to face every
> newcomer with new capacity already geared into a great organiza-
> tion, having the advantage of experience, trade connections, and

---

[5] *U.S.* v. *Aluminum Company of America,* 148 F.2d 416 (2d Cir., 1945).

the elite of personnel. . . . No monopolist monopolizes unconscious of what he is doing.[6]

In sum, what the court apparently held in *Alcoa* was that a company with substantial market power is guilty of violating Section 2 of the Sherman Act unless the company could not have avoided the possession of market power, yet the only means by which Alcoa could have avoided the power it possessed in 1945 was to have grown less rapidly in aluminum production in the preceding thirty-three years, during which period it grew at a compounded annual rate of approximately 20 per cent. Under the hypothetical tax-rebate schedule used for illustrative purposes in Chapter 3, Alcoa would have earned gross annual rebates of 4 per cent and net rebates of 3 per cent. Growth rewards of this magnitude would unquestionably have induced Alcoa even more "progressively to embrace each new opportunity as it opened," and in consequence to grow even more rapidly than it did, but it would have been no less guilty of violating the Sherman Act.

The judicial doctrine that "vigorous growth can be the root of guilt" established in *Alcoa* led to other Section 2 prosecutions. After the *Alcoa* decision the Department of Justice initiated a civil action against the United Shoe Machinery Corporation. Judge Wyzanski's decision in *United Shoe* parallels that of Judge Hand's in *Alcoa*:

> United's power does not rest on predatory practices. Probably few monopolists could produce a record so free from any taint of that kind of wrong doing. The violation with which United is now charged depends not on moral considerations, but on solely economic considerations. United is denied the right to exercise effective control of the market by business policies that are not the inevitable consequences of its capacities or its natural advantages.[7]

---

[6] *Ibid.*, pp. 431, 432.

[7] *U.S.* v. *United Shoe Machinery Corp.*, 110 F. Supp. 295, 345 (D. Mass., 1953).

The *Alcoa* decision precipitated other antitrust actions, but the two cases illustrate sufficiently well the possible conflict between present antitrust doctrine and the proposed growth bonus scheme, namely, firm growth, although unaccompanied by predatory practices, resulting in substantial market control is vulnerable to prosecution under Section 2 of the Sherman Act. Accordingly, a growth scheme which rewards firm growth will very likely have one of the two following consequences, possibly a combination of both: either the prevailing *Alcoa* doctrine will cause the scheme to induce less growth of business firms than it otherwise would, or antitrust prosecutions of the this variety will increase. These consequences would ensue unless a logical case could be made that the growth scheme would lead such firms to grow in other product lines at the expense of growth in those lines they already produce. Such a case can probably be made for firms producing products having only an average, or below average, growth potential; they earn zero or negative net growth bonuses and therefore have a strong incentive to enter industries with high potential growth rates. Furthermore, such new entrants into growth industries may in some cases prevent a single firm from rising to a position of dominant market power. In these cases the growth scheme may well tend to reduce monopoly and in consequence serve to prevent violations of Section 2. But for growth industries that follow the pattern of aluminum the constraining forces of the *Alcoa* doctrine and the proposed growth bonus incentive system operate in opposing directions.

4. Patents and growth. In recent years, especially over the past two decades, there has developed a trend away from exclusive use of patents. Three factors account for this trend: (1) manufacturing firms in possession of patents have demonstrated an increased willingness to license other firms, probably because the scale at which many modern inventions can be profitably exploited greatly exceeds the resources and scale economies of a single enterprise; (2) there has been a substantial increase in the number of firms engaged almost entirely in developing and patenting new technology, leaving manufacturing to their licensees; and (3) the courts have resolved far more conflicts between the exclusive use of patent rights and Section 2 of the Sherman Act in favor of the latter than they did in the early decades of antitrust.[8] Compulsory licensing is the most frequently employed remedy in such cases. Because much economic growth is attributable to the development and dissemination of new technology, this trend away from the exclusive use of patented inventions has presumably accelerated the rate of economic growth.

Were patent accounting methods not so complex and imprecise, there would be very little reason, on balance, to suppose that the proposed growth scheme would appreciably affect this trend one way or the other. Because the scheme measures growth in terms of value added at the firm level, inventing firms presumably would have an added incentive to generate a larger share of the value added for the patented process or product themselves; that is, they would have an incentive to withhold licenses from other firms. However, potential licensees would have an equally strong incentive to bid up royalty rates to a level that compensated the patentee for the profits and growth bonuses it would lose through licensing. Accordingly, licensing presumably would go on as in the absence of the growth scheme, but at higher royalty rates.

However, the difficulties of adapting patent accounting to the value-added concept may tend to reduce the volume of licensing. Business firms typically treat royalty receipts as

[8] George E. Frost, S. Chesterfield Oppenheim, and Neil F. Twomey, *Patent, Trade-Mark, and Copyright Journal of Research and Education* (June, 1957), pp. 135-36.

"other income" rather than sales and absorb research and development expenditures, especially since the 1952 amendment to the Internal Revenue Code, in current operating expenses. They follow this procedure in part because it is virtually impossible to segregate revenues and costs on a basis of individual patents. Thus the conventional calculation of value added (sales — material costs) excludes the revenue side of patentable inventive activity altogether and in the process deprives the patenting firm of its eligibility to receive growth bonuses on its patent-licensing business. Confronted with this prospect, inventing firms would have a strong incentive to refuse licenses to others and manufacture the entire patent-protected output, even though they may run greater risks of prosecution under the Sherman Act in doing so.

There are several possible ways whereby these accounting difficulties and their prospective attendant licensing policies may be remedied. The simplest remedy would be to treat the sale of the rights to use patented technology, which in essence licensing arrangements are, just as the sale of any other commodity. Annual value added quantities for firms could then be calculated from the formula: "(Accounting sales plus royalty income) minus (costs of product material plus costs of inventive activity material)." [9] This way of meeting the difficulty raises the question of what price deflator is applicable to royalty revenues.[10] Though there is no completely satisfactory means of meeting this problem, it is probably possible to adapt patent-licensing revenues and costs to the value-added concept in ways that will not seriously interfere with either antitrust policy or the proposed growth scheme. For one reason, by far the great majority of patent-holding firms' patent revenues and costs comprise only a small percentage of total

---

[9] All in constant prices.

[10] Material cost applicable to patentable research poses no special problems, aside from the fact that it comprises a relatively small fraction of the costs involved.

sales and costs; this small percentage could be adjusted by the same indexes applied to the firm's principal product sales and cost items without seriously affecting the results.[11] For another reason, licensing contracts usually stipulate royalty rates of x per unit of product or y per cent of the price at which the licensee sells the product. When expressed as x per unit the price of the sale of technology is like any other price and could be weighted by the share of the firm's total revenue attributable to licensing. When expressed as y per cent of the sales price it can quickly and easily be converted to a price series. The licensee could be permitted to treat royalty payments just as he treats material costs on the grounds that it is a payment to another firm in an earlier stage of fabrication. This way of handling patent revenue and cost items, although not entirely satisfactory, should reduce the area of conflict between the growth scheme and prevailing antitrust policy toward patents by allowing patent-holding firms to share in the rewards of growth by licensing.

5. Predatory practices and firm growth: the Clayton and Federal Trade Commission Acts. The test of illegality under the Sherman Act hangs on the possession of substantial market power. The Federal Trade Commission and Clayton Acts are for the most part directed toward specific business practices which may tend toward monopoly or to injure competition. They make illegal such practices as price discrimination, tying-sales, exclusive dealing contracts, mergers, and unfair methods of competition which have the prohibited effects. And various predatory practices are illegal under certain provisions of these acts and the Sherman Act.

---

[11] That is, if the expression $(P_{t+n}/P_t) = 105$, where P is the price of the product sold, it could be assumed that 5 per cent of any measured increase in royalty revenues was attributable to price increases and accordingly deflated by an index of 105.

If for no reason other than that these statutory provisions contemplate actions in markets characterized by only modest levels of market power in the hands of individual firms, they are addressed more to the problem of firm growth at the expense of rivals than to growth in response to increased total demand. The conventional profit incentive alone provides sufficient stimulus to these practices to produce a large number of legal actions each year under the above statutory provisions. It seems fairly clear that the growth bonus scheme would make the incentive to engage in such practices even greater. The most promising means of growth for a firm in possession of considerably less than half of a relevant market is to employ those strategies which promote its sales at the expense of rivals. It is generally conceded that larger firms can employ them more successfully than small ones. It is therefore reasonable to conclude that the growth scheme will accelerate the use of discriminatory pricing, tying contracts, exclusive dealing arrangements, unfair methods of competition, and the large array of predatory practices firms use to increase their sales at the expense of rivals.

However, the fact that the prospect of growth bonuses may lead to greater use of such strategies does not add up to an irreconcilable conflict between the ends of antitrust policy and the growth scheme. The growth scheme is designed to stimulate net economic growth although it proposes to measure and reward growth at the firm level. Antitrust policy toward these strategies is designed primarily to frustrate "unfair" attempts at reapportioning existing demand among firms rather than to stifle net growth.[12] Adoption of the proposed growth scheme,

---

[12] This does not mean that certain of the statutory provisions leave growth unaffected. In fact, it is frequently urged that strict application of the Robinson-Patman Act stifles some competitive growth. This is a problem of antitrust reform rather than of conflict between antitrust policy and the proposed growth scheme.

or any similar scheme, would unquestionably require more vigorous administration of antitrust policy in this area, but there is little reason to suppose that this would, in turn, conflict with the scheme's objective of stimulating net growth. On the contrary, it can be argued rather persuasively that more restricted use of business policies aimed at reducing the sales of rivals may lead to greater use of business policies which result in net economic growth; closing off the socially less beneficial avenues of firm growth may very well increase the traffic over more beneficial routes.

The possible impact of the proposed growth scheme on merger and vertical integration merits somewhat more detailed analysis. Merger is an especially clear case of firm growth which does not immediately result in net growth; it is simply a transfer of productive capacity from the acquired to the acquiring firm. In many cases merger may be regarded as a means of *avoiding* net growth; acquiring firms often substitute acquisitions for new plant construction. Section 7 of the Clayton Act, in outlawing mergers which tend substantially to lessen competition, is designed primarily to prevent industrial concentration, but it also stimulates economic growth; new plant construction is often substituted for those mergers the law prevents.

If it could be assumed that in any potential merger the expectations for growth of the acquired firm are unaffected by merger, the proposed growth scheme would raise no new problems for Section 7 administration. The scheme, as stated elsewhere in this book, excludes growth by merger from value-added computations. The exclusion of merger would presumably cause the substitution of some new plant construction for mergers which existing incentives would bring about because expanding firms would receive credit for the "build-up" period. Furthermore, if merger did not affect the prospects for growth of the acquired firm under consideration, any incentive to buy, which the potential acquirer may have, is offset by an equally strong incentive on the part of the potential seller not to sell. Consider, for example, a situation where a $900 million "value added" firm with a growth rate of 4 per cent contemplates acquiring a $1 million "value added" firm with a growth rate of 20 per cent. The tax and rebate schedules for the separate firms and the two firms combined would be as follows:

Firm	Per Cent of Increase in Value Added	Per Cent of Additional Tax	Per Cent of Rebate	Net Per Cent of Value Added and Amount as Tax (−) or Rebate (+)
$900 million acquirer	4.0	1.0	0.8	−0.2 (−$1.8 million)
$100 million acquired	20.0	1.0	4.0	+3.0 (+$3.0 million)
$1 billion acquirer-acquired merged	5.6	1.0	1.12	+0.12 (+$1.2 million)

Through merger the acquiring firm could increase, in years following the merger, its net rebate from −$1.8 million to +$1.2 million or by exactly the $3 million in net rebates which the acquired firm would give up. The discounted value of the annual stream of $3 million would presumably be reflected in the price at which the selling firm would sell. The proposed growth scheme, under these assumptions, provides no additional incentive for merger.

However, the assumption that merger does not alter the expected growth rate of the acquired firm's operations is highly questionable. Firms that acquire other firms usually have plans for expanding them; firms that sell to other firms often do so because they have not had satisfactory growth rates, or because of a host of other reasons which imply prospects of little growth, or perhaps because they anticipate a decline in sales or a permanent exit from the line of business altogether.[13] The accumulated body of facts on merger suggests that the acquired firm has prospects for a substantially higher growth rate as a participant in merger than as an independent firm. In view of the proposed growth bonuses, this means that such firms can increase their revenue earning capacity by merging. The proposed growth scheme would probably increase the volume of mergers, even those which may have the legally prohibited effects of "tending substantially to lessen competition." Whether it would provide a new incentive for merger would depend on the ratio of "build-up" growth to the growth expected to follow the acquisition. If the latter is large relative to the former, the growth scheme would provide a new inducement to merger and hence would call for more vigorous administration of Section 7 of the Clayton Act. In contrast, if "build-up" growth possibilities are significant, the prospective growth bonuses may induce firms to substitute internal expansion for merger and thereby reduce the volume of Section 7 litigations. And since "build-up" growth potential is greatest when the prospective acquired firm is already large, it may reasonably be concluded that the proposed growth scheme would reduce the number of instances where firms acquire large firms, that is, instances where the probability of a substantial lessening of competition is the greatest.

A recent merger decision serves to illustrate how the deterrent effect of Section 7 and the incentive of growth bonuses may operate in opposite directions on the business firm. In 1956 Brown Shoe Company, a shoe manufacturer, acquired Kenney Shoe Company, a family shoe distribution chain. Brown Shoe manufactured and Kenney Shoe distributed less

---

[13] See J. Keith Butters, John Lintner, and W. L. Cary, *Effects of Taxation on Corporate Mergers* (Cambridge: Harvard University Press, 1951).

than 5 per cent of the shoes sold in the United States. The alleged purpose of the merger was to effect certain economies which would reduce the retail price of family shoes, thus permitting the merged firm to grow more rapidly than either could grow independently. Although much of the firm's growth would be made at the expense of rival shoe manufacturers and distributors, some would presumably have been net growth. The incentive for the merger, and for the post-merger growth, would have been even more compelling under the proposed growth scheme.

In 1959 the court declared the Brown-Kenney merger a violation of Section 7 largely for the same reasons the firms merged.[14] The court found that in fact the merger would lead to the growth of the two companies, and that much of this growth would result from the lower prices the combination could afford to charge. But it found also that much of the growth would be at the expense of unintegrated rivals. Hence, for the first time in a litigation under the 1950 antimerger statute, the court equated substantial injury to competitors with a substantial lessening of competition. A system of growth bonuses would very likely lead to an increase in Section 7 cases of this type.

Analysis of the possible effects of the proposed growth scheme on vertical integration involves essentially the same considerations as those involved in the analysis of merger, especially where vertical integration is attained through merger. A firm's entry into a preceding or succeeding stage of fabrication wil be governed by all the familiar business incentives and, in addition, by the prospects for earning growth bonuses. Furthermore, whether it enters by internal expansion or by merger will depend largely on the ratio of "build-up" growth to expected post-merger growth.

---

[14] *U.S.* v. *Brown Shoe Co.,* 179 F. Supp. 721 (E.D. Mo., 1959).

Because the proposed growth bonus scheme rewards growth in value added, and because vertical integration is generally one of the simplest means whereby a firm may increase its value added, it can be concluded with virtual certainty that the scheme would intensify efforts on the part of firms to integrate vertically. However, general increases in the level of vertical integration throughout the economy could lead either to an increase or a decrease in competition and hence could either aggravate or reduce the problems of antitrust policy. For example, if many of the large number of firms engaged in the manufacture of mixed fertilizer were to integrate backward to the mining of phosphate rock, potash, and sulfur, each of which is produced by a few large firms, competition would be increased. However, if the "big-three" automobile manufacturers were suddenly to start manufacturing all their parts and accessories, industries now comprising many competitors would eventually become highly concentrated in the hands of these large firms. These examples serve only to point out that the effect of vertical integration on competition, the aspect of vertical integration with which antitrust policy is concerned, depends on its source, direction, and the prevailing levels of concentration in specific markets connecting successive stages of fabrication.

It can be argued, indeed has often been argued,[15] that vertical integration usually occurs through the process of large, financially strong companies buying up their smaller and weaker suppliers and customers. The argument's principal appeal lies in the fact that vertical integration along these lines is at least possible, whereas integration in the opposite direction may be virtually impossible. For example, General Motors obviously has the financial resources to buy into spark-

---

[15] *Cf.* Fritz Machlup and Martha Taber, "Bilateral Monopoly, Successive Monopoly, and Vertical Integration," *Economica* (May, 1960), pp. 101-102.

plug manufacturing or the retailing of automobiles if it should decide that to do so would be to its financial advantage; a small spark-plug manufacturer would find it nearly impossible to duplicate the facilities of General Motors, or even American Motors.

However, there is little reason to believe that the proposed growth scheme would, on balance, give large firms an added stimulus to invade sectors now in the hands of small suppliers and customers. Small business units tend to dominate fabrication and distribution stages characterized by small-scale economies. Such stages are therefore not a promising source of growth for large manufacturing firms, certainly not as promising a source as other lines of enterprise characterized by significant economies of scale. Hence, the likelihood is at least as great that the proposed growth scheme would lead large firms to invade industrial sectors dominated by other large firms as it is that it will lead them to take over sectors dominated by small business. The scheme provides business firms, whether large or small, with an additional incentive to grow in terms of value added. They presumably will pursue the most promising of the available alternative sources of growth. There are no logical grounds for concluding that the prospects of growth bonuses would make competition-reducing (concentration-increasing) vertical integration a more promising avenue to growth than it already is or relatively more promising than other sources of firm growth.

6. The growth scheme as a stimulus to competitive growth. Up to this point analysis has centered on possible conflicts between particular antitrust doctrines and the proposed system of incentives for growth. However, certain broad objectives of both the proposed growth scheme and antitrust policy complement each other. The most difficult problem confronting antitrust agencies is the tight-knit oligopoly. Under tacit agreement oligopolists often have the effect of monopoly but generate none of the legal evidence of conspiracy. The growth scheme provides an incentive for oligopolists to grow, whether at the expense of rival oligopolists or in ways which increase net economic growth. In some cases the incentive should be sufficiently strong to eliminate most of the effects of tacit agreement. In the process an oligopolist may occasionally violate the *Alcoa* doctrine, and may frequently be led to violate certain provisions of the Clayton and Federal Trade Commission Acts. However, even in this event more vigorous growth effort would have resulted in the substitution of relatively simple antitrust problems for the complex and difficult problem of tacitly conspiring oligopolists.

Moreover, an effective growth incentive should lead to some substitution of growth for monopolistic policies. Professor Hicks has suggested that the primary reward of monopoly is a "quiet life," but it may be added that the cost of monopoly is eternal vigil. The preservation of quasi-monopolistic control requires the expenditure of managerial effort. In the dynamic and multi-product economy of the United States there must exist many situations where the proposed growth bonuses would raise the marginal returns on managerial effort to grow above the marginal returns on effort to preserve existing market shares. And where growth effort is directed toward entering a different industry, it thereby reduces the market power of those firms already there. The ways in which the growth scheme may help solve antitrust problems such as these may not be predictable with precision, but it can be reasonably predicted that the scheme will help for their solution.

7. Summary and conclusions. A financial incentive for firm growth may aggravate the problems of antitrust law administration in at least three ways: (1) The proposed bonus scheme makes no distinction between growth as such and growth which results in substantial market power. Market power is itself a sufficiently great incentive to have precipitated numerous lawsuits under Section 2 of the Sherman Act. When the prospective bonus pay-offs for growth are added to the normal rewards of market control, the number of cases will very likely increase. Moreover, where growth results in substantial market control, even though market control per se may not have been the stimulus to growth, the antitrust doctrine laid down in the *Alcoa* decision may limit the effectiveness of the growth incentive. Innocent growth which results in substantial market control, under the *Alcoa* doctrine, may be illegal monopoly. (2) The various business strategies which firms use to promote growth at the expense of rivals would undoubtedly be used more often and more vigorously under a system of growth incentives. Many such strategies, including unfair methods of competition, tying-sales, exclusive dealings and price-discrimination which tends substantially to lessen competition, are illegal under the Clayton and Federal Trade Commission Acts. Cases involving these statutes are already numerous, and may be expected to increase in volume under the proposed growth bonus scheme. (3) The growth scheme will probably lead to an increase in certain types of illegal mergers.

The conflicts between the two policies are not beyond reconciliation. In the final analysis they mean simply that the proposed growth scheme would cost society something in terms of an increase in resources allocated to antitrust law administration required to preserve antitrust policy as it is presently construed. To the extent that the growth scheme furthers the objectives of antitrust policy in other areas, it provides a partial compensation for these added costs. The scheme should help to solve the problems of tacitly conspiring oligopolists and should induce firms to enter some industries and reduce existing levels of market concentration. Finally, initiation of the growth scheme would impose on Congress and the courts an obligation to clarify some of the uncertainties concerning the legal status of business size, market power, mergers, and pricing practices. Such clarification would in the long run reduce the costs of antitrust law administration. The costs of the growth scheme would therefore not be as great as the three areas of conflict might suggest.

The areas of conflict themselves can be dealt with in a number of ways. No newly initiated policy is expected to operate in a legal and institutional vacuum. Some banks presumably could grow by robbing other banks, but this is scarcely a sufficient reason for repealing existing laws against theft. One means of dealing with such conflicts is to let the growth scheme operate under existing antitrust constraints, especially since they do not appear to constrain prohibitively. There are precedents for this solution. For example, tax laws enacted after 1940 are alleged to have increased significantly the volume of mergers. But the courts have not yet recognized the tax incentive as a legal defense in a merger case and hence have left the prospect of a lawsuit as a constraint on the full operation of the tax incentive. Alternatively, antitrust policy could be modified so as to reduce the area of conflict between it and the proposed growth scheme. Historically, Congress and the courts generally have bent the antitrust laws to accommodate new and important policies. No doubt both would take a few steps in this direction even though no explicit recommendation be made that they do so. In any case there are no persuasive reasons for proposing repeal of the *Alcoa* doctrine and specific provisions of the Clayton and Federal Trade Commission Acts until the details of the constraints they impose on the proposed growth scheme have been more fully revealed. The conflicts are not, a priori, beyond the reach of modest judicial compromise.

· 8 ·

Economic Expansion,
External Solvency,
and the Gains from Trade

STERIE T. BEZA AND GARDNER PATTERSON

The purpose of this chapter is to explore the impact of a more rapid rate of economic expansion on the foreign trade and payments position of the United States.

We must note at the outset that there are many factors other than the rate of economic expansion, that affect a country's external position. We do not underestimate the significance of these other factors and realize that they may often be so powerful as to swamp the effects of an increase in the rate of economic growth. Nonetheless, the task set in this book is to evaluate the particular forces that emanate from more rapid growth.

We find that an acceleration of output is likely to create some problems for us in the international economic sphere and that these difficulties are associated with the fact of an increase in the rate of growth rather than with the particular proposal set forth in Chapter 3. Indeed, because the proposal advanced in this book relies on tax incentives it will create far fewer international economic problems for us than those proposals which stress monetary ease as a means for stimulating economic expansion.

There are two major kinds of international economic effects that warrant elaboration and discussion: alteration of a country's balance of payments position and changes in the "real" gains derived from trade.

Balance of payments problems are monetary in nature and are generally considered to be short-run phenomena. To say this is not to imply that payments deficits and surpluses never stem from real factors such as changes in tastes and changes in the rate of growth but rather that they usually appear as phenomena to which attention must be paid because of the existence of separate national currencies. It is the changes in a nation's holdings of gold and foreign exchange reserves that are usually used to measure a country's deficit or surplus in its balance of payments. Balance of payments problems are short run in the sense that a country cannot continue indefinitely to run into balance of payments difficulties; eventually it will exhaust its gold and foreign exchange reserves. It also follows that continuing balance of payments surpluses are precluded inasmuch as these either drain the reserves of other countries or increase their foreign liabilities beyond tolerable limits. It is in the long run inescapable that a country achieve equilibrium in its external payments position. Of course, this does not preclude the possibility of a series of difficult and sometimes seemingly intractable short-run problems as, for example, those faced by western Europe after World War II or by the United States in recent years.

Terms of trade problems are real in nature, though they may stem from monetary phenomena, and are not necessarily short run. In a closed economy, one that is not involved in foreign trade, each gain in real output is at the same time a gain in the real income of the residents of the country. But if the economy is open, that is, it engages in foreign trade, allowance has to be made for the possibility that the two growth rates, of real output and of real income, will diverge because the ratio at which exports exchange for imports is altered.

An increase in domestic real output that causes a *deterioration* in the terms of trade (export prices fall relative to import prices) will result in a gain in real income that is smaller than the advance in output. Part of the real output increase goes to foreigners as a larger quantity of exports is required to pay for each unit of imports. Conversely, an increase in domestic real output attended by an improvement in the terms of trade results in real income advances that exceed the growth in real output.

1. Balance of payments aspects. We turn first to a consideration of the balance of payments aspects of an increase in the rate of economic expansion in the United States. To simplify the exposition we assume that prior to the acceleration of the rate of economic growth in the United States we are in approximate external balance with the rest of the world. We also assume that the current rates of growth in other countries, whatever these rates may be, are maintained except to the extent that they may be affected by what happens in the United States. We are superimposing on the existing situation an improvement in the rate of economic expansion in the United States and asking what impact this will have on our external payments position. It should be noted that even if our rate of growth is increased, there may still be other countries whose rates of economic expansion continue to exceed ours.

Unless and until experience proves otherwise, we must expect that implementation of a proposal such as that offered here will result in roughly the same improvement in the rate of increase of productivity in all sectors of the economy.[1] That is, we shall assume that if productivity for the economy as a whole increases by x per cent, then each industry experiences an x per cent increase in productivity.

It also seems likely that in the American economy, in the absence of a special effort by the Government, any improvement in productivity and output will at least be matched by increases in money incomes, with the result that the prices of our exports and import-competing goods will not decline. Indeed, it is probable that the monopolistic pressures of both business and labor unions aimed at improving their incomes will result in money incomes exceeding improvements in productivity. However, similar forces are also at work in most of the rest of the world and it is not unreasonable to anticipate that with a steady improvement in real output, we in the United States should be able to contain price increases sufficiently to prevent them from outpacing, on balance, those of the rest of the world. Indeed, one of the major advantages of the specific proposal advanced in this book is that it does not rely on inflation for its effectiveness. If this proves to be the case, the more rapid growth will not produce any "price effects" that would disturb the initial trade position with respect to the balance of payments. There will be no price incentive for domestic producers and consumers to substitute imports for domestically produced commodities or vice versa, nor will there be any reason for foreigners to purchase more or fewer American goods because of price differentials.

However, even in this "ideal" case, there are income and

---

[1] "Productivity," as we shall use it, is the ratio of the output of goods and services to the input of resources. An improvement in the rate of increase of productivity means that output increases relative to the input. We presume that an increase in the rate of growth of real output will involve an increase in productivity.

output effects that we must anticipate will operate to worsen the United States balance of payments position. An improvement in productivity and output that is matched by an equivalent increase in money income will result in an increase in the quantity of goods demanded by residents of the United States, both by producers who will need more raw materials and finished goods used in the production process, and by consumers whose higher incomes will induce a rise in their expenditures. These demands will be for import-type and export-type goods and services as well as for items that do not enter into foreign trade.

But growth also will result in increased supplies of all, or nearly all, of these various kinds of goods. The net effect of all this on the balance of payments will depend on the relative strengths of these two forces: the increase in supply and the increase in demand for goods and services. But if the quantity demanded and supplied by Americans of each major category of goods rises in proportion to the increase in real income or output, then the balance of payments will tend to show a deficit. That is, for those commodities in which our consumption exceeds domestic output, with the difference being made up through imports, an equal percentage increase in quantities demanded and supplied must result in an increase in imports. However, there will be no equivalent increase in foreign demand for those goods of which we are net exporters. The consequence will be a balance of payments deficit which must be met by the exportation of gold, or by a worsening of our net reserve position as foreigners add to their dollar balances, or, more likely, by some of both.

For more favorable results on our balance of payments it is necessary that the increase in output of import-type goods, brought about by the productivity improvement, exceed the increase in demand for those goods. If, as we have been assuming, the growth is in fact uniformly distributed throughout the economy, this result can occur only if the pattern and strength of domestic demand is such that the quantity of import goods demanded rises by a smaller percentage than the improvement in productivity.

One would expect that, in an economy as diverse as ours, there will be cases in which the increase in demand for some products will be more than offset by increases in domestic output, thereby reducing the quantity of imports demanded. However, we find nothing that encourages the expectation that this kind of outcome will be widespread. In many instances there is no domestic supply at all of goods and services that are close substitutes for imports, for example, of bananas or a holiday in Europe. In many other instances it can be argued plausibly that the demand for many consumer goods which we import (for example, luxury consumer goods) will continue to increase, as they have in recent years, at a still more rapid rate than the improvement in our real income. There is some evidence that we have already reached, or will soon reach, a standard of living at which further improvements will result in more than proportionate increases in consumers' demand for high quality, distinctive design, and non-mass produced types of goods which are commonly associated with imports. For a great many industrial raw materials, the United States is already a net importer, and we expect that increases in demand associated with more rapid growth will at least parallel the increases in national output. It follows that we can expect increases in these imports. Moreover, for several important industrial raw materials, the United States may well be facing costs of production that are increasing more rapidly at home than abroad; if so, this is a special price effect that can be expected to induce larger imports.

But, it can be asked, will there not occur an expansion in

our exports? A commonly held view is that a higher rate of growth will throw up an increasing number of fresh and interesting products which will improve the external payments position by adding new products to the export list or by replacing certain imports. This will, of course, happen from time to time, but neither the particular proposal offered here nor others that have been advanced provide special incentives for developing *new* products. We see no reason, therefore, to expect this to constitute a steady and important source of relief to the foreign payments position of the United States.

Similarly, it is open to one to hope that an acceleration in the rate of advance of productivity in the United States will not, as we have assumed, be spread equally over the entire economy but will induce particularly large increases in productivity in those sectors of the economy which produce import-competing or export-type goods. If this were to happen, one would expect the prices of these types of goods to decline relatively to the general price level. The consequence would probably be an improvement in our international financial position. However, we see no reason why a more rapid rate of growth in general, or the growth that would be stimulated by this particular proposal, would necessarily produce these kinds of systematic biases. It is equally likely, or unlikely, that increases in productivity would be particularly modest in those sectors producing foreign-traded goods, in which case our balance of payments problems would be more serious than we foresee.

It is also possible that the particular proposal advanced in this book for stimulating growth will lead to higher interest rates, particularly since the proposal rests on tax incentives. If long-term interest rates rise, foreign long-term investment in the United States will be encouraged, and United States investment abroad will be discouraged. The result, for a time at least, will be to strengthen our external payments position. Such benefits, however, will probably be minor. First, the difference in interest rates between the United States and abroad that are likely to be involved are small compared to the other considerations which dictate foreign investment decisions. Second, balance of payments relief on this score is at the price of reduced future receipts from income on our foreign investments and of enlarged United States payments on investment income account for foreign investments. To the extent that the proposal leads to higher short-term interest rates, there will be clear and quick benefits to the balance of payments, but once lenders of short-term funds have adjusted to the new pattern of interest rates, one would not expect further large changes in the total amount of interest-sensitive balances held by foreigners in the United States.

The upshot of all this is that we expect a sharp improvement in the rate of economic growth in the United States to cause some balance of payments difficulties. However, the United States, as compared with most nations, does not rely heavily on either imports or exports, and so any resulting balance of payments deficit will not be large in terms of American total production. But even if it were no more than one-half of 1 per cent of our GNP, the problem might be a serious one indeed; the record of the past few years shows that a deficit of $2-4 billion a year can create problems that *must* be resolved. They simply cannot be "lived with" as some other national problems of this dollar dimension can. A deficit of these dimensions could quite easily result from a doubling of the rate of economic growth in the United States.

If such an imbalance can be neither ignored nor tolerated, then anyone recommending a faster rate of growth must consider means for removing the deficit. As we see it, there are two general kinds of policies available. Either we must resort to increasing the barriers to imports and other foreign payments, or we must undertake policies aimed at changing the price of American goods and services relative to foreign ones.

Stiffer import duties or more stringent quantitative restrictions on imports could remove the external payments deficit. The economic price, however, would be high, for such a policy fosters inefficient production in that it almost always transfers the locus of production from lower to higher cost areas. Inefficient production is in direct conflict with the central purpose of a program of accelerated growth. If other nations retaliated, and past experience suggests that this would be probable, the economic price for them and for us would, of course, increase. Furthermore, any such retreat by the United States from her long-established policies of favoring an expansion of multilateral non-discriminatory trade will be costly in terms of her international political objectives. And, as was said in Chapter 1, among the reasons favoring efforts to increase the rate of growth is the need to strengthen our international political leadership. For all these reasons we would rule out this "solution."

Turning to measures designed to make our exports more attractive by giving them some price advantages over those of foreigners, we find two major methods. The first is the device of altering the exchange rate. It is difficult to consider this seriously as an adjustment device open to the United States so long as the international monetary system relies on the dollar as a reserve currency. This country is now the most important international reserve center and the responsibilities this carries with it, under present arrangements, include the making of some real sacrifices, if needed, to maintain a fixed exchange rate. The mere possibility of a change in the exchange rate would induce many foreign holders of dollar balances to exchange them for gold, and the probable consequence of this would be a major deterioration in the world's international reserve position, thus creating new obstacles for expanded trade and for the greater efficiency that is implied in more trade. If the international monetary system were so reorganized that there existed the equivalent of an international central bank to take over the international reserve-creating process now performed by national banking systems and currencies, the dollar and the pound sterling in particular, then it would be open to the United States to resort to the relatively simple device of moderate exchange rate variations to cope with external payments difficulties. Until such an institution is available, however, devaluation of the dollar is an inappropriate way of dealing with a balance of payments deficit of the kind and of the dimensions that an accelerated rate of economic growth might bring about.

A second method of adjustment to a balance of payments deficit that might arise from our accelerated growth would be to pursue such domestic policies as would result in our prices falling relative to those abroad. More specifically, the indicated policy here is not merely to keep the ratio of increases in money incomes to productivity increases at as favorable a rate as those in the rest of the world but to restrain the growth of money incomes in such a manner that prices in the United States fall relative to prices abroad. If foreign prices remain stable, it will be necessary to hold increases in our money incomes to less than the increases in productivity and real output. In the light of the various considerations outlined in Chapter 6, we do not believe that such a policy would be likely to be implemented. Fortunately, such a herculean effort will probably not be called for. It is likely that foreign prices will more or less persistently rise. In this event it may be sufficient if the United States succeeds in holding the rise in money incomes to a rate equal to that of the growth in productivity. Even this will not be easy. Fortunately, however, the amount by which United States prices have to fall relative to foreign prices, in the interest of external balance, is rather small. The reason for this is primarily that on both the import and export side, United States foreign trade encompasses a wide range of products, many of which are both produced and consumed at home; the result is that comparatively small changes in relative prices will move many commodities from the non-traded to traded categories and, indeed, even from imports to exports and vice-versa. In other words, given a reasonable passage of time, relatively small changes in United States prices compared to foreign prices will bring about large changes in the value of trade, and it is the latter which will constitute the necessary adjustment.

The foregoing considerations indicate that a program of accelerated economic growth in the United States may well involve balance of payments adjustments that impose significant costs to the economy. If we rely on raising barriers to imports, the cost is inefficient production. If other countries avoid inflation and, as a consequence, we are forced to pursue very stringent policies on the growth of money income, we may run into conflict with domestic employment objectives, given present trade union policies on money wages. If, finally, we turn to exchange rate variations, the cost, under present arrangements, must be reckoned in terms of destroying much of the world's reserves or, if new international financial institutions are established, in foregoing some of the many benefits which accrue to nations serving as international financial centers.

If other nations permit at least moderate inflation, our problems will be eased as they would be if our growth were characterized by a systematic bias in productivity improvements in favor of the import-competing or export sectors of our economy. We may hope for these things, but it would be unwise, in calculating the rewards and costs of accelerated growth, to rely on the advent of such fortuitous events.

2. The terms of trade problem. Before we can denote an increase in real output as an increase in real income, we must take account of the terms on which our goods and services are exchanged with those of foreigners. Expansion of a country's real output is likely to affect its demand for imports and its supply of exports and, consequently, not only total payments and receipts, the *balance of payments,* but also the relationship between export prices and import prices, that is, the *terms of trade*. If an increase in domestic real output, whether fostered by the growth proposal under consideration or by something else, brings about a worsening in the terms of trade (a fall in export prices relative to import prices), then the gain in real output will automatically have to be shared with foreigners as a larger quantity of exports is required to pay for each unit of imports. In contrast, if the increases in domestic real output are accompanied by an improvement in the terms of trade, then the real income of the United States will rise more rapidly than the growth in real output.

We have argued above that unless we are the happy beneficiaries of fortuitous events, it is likely that a program of accelerated economic growth in the United States will lead to balance of payments problems which will necessitate remedial policies. Among the most likely of such events are price inflation abroad exceeding that at home and systematic biases in United States productivity improvements in favor of import-competing and export goods.

If we are rescued from balance of payments embarrassments by foreign price increases, then it follows that our terms of trade will worsen and that we cannot keep for ourselves all the real gain in output. If the productivity improvement is especially high in American export industries, then the decline of export prices relative to other prices (both at home and abroad) may make it possible to avoid balance of payments difficulties, but on the real side we again have to contend with a deterioration of the terms of trade.[2] However, if the productivity gains are concentrated in import-competing industries, then it is the prices of these goods which one would expect to fall relative to others; hence, the likely result is that we would suffer less serious or even no balance of payments problems and would even enjoy an increase in real income larger than the increase in our output.

If, as we have already asserted, such fortuitous events cannot be relied upon year in and year out to meet all our anticipated balance of payments problems, then action will be needed by the United States either to restrain the growth of money incomes to a rate less than we would choose for a closed economy or to alter the exchange rate. The use of either policy, or a combination of the two, must be expected to bring about some deterioration in the ratio at which we exchange our exports for imports since the balance of payments adjustment process involves increasing the quantity of goods and services sold abroad relative to the quantity of purchases from foreigners.

We conclude that accelerated growth will cost the nation something in the sense that part of the gain from expanded output will spill over to the benefit of foreigners—a consequence which may, incidentally, have advantages on foreign-policy grounds. We also believe, however, that this cost is likely to be small for, as we argued earlier, comparatively small decreases in the prices of American goods relative to the prices

---

[2] It warrants emphasis here that this is not a justification for restricting trade. In terms of inputs the benefit from trade is greater than non-trade even though it is less than it would have been had the terms not gone against us.

of foreign goods will probably bring about large changes in the value of our international trade. It must also be emphasized that these small changes in the terms of trade will have an almost negligible effect upon real income because of the small part that foreign trade plays in our national income. Assume, for example, that the rate of productivity increase is raised from the present 2½ per cent per annum to 5 per cent per annum and that the ratio of imports to national income increases by one-quarter, or to about .06. Without any deterioration in the terms of trade, real income would rise by 5 per cent per annum, 2½ per cent above the initial rate. Suppose, however, that the improvement in productivity leads for some time to a 3 per cent per annum deterioration in the terms of trade, an extreme assumption in our view. This would reduce the per annum growth in real income from 5 per cent to about 4.8 per cent, or, to put it another way, of the 2½ per cent *addition* to productivity and output, over 2.3 per cent would accrue to the United States and less than .2 per cent would accrue to foreigners. This is a possible cost of economic growth that is usually forgotten, but it is a small one and pales into insignificance when compared with the advantages of a faster rate of growth that were outlined in Chapter 1.

3. Economic growth abroad. Up to now we have assumed that foreign countries will continue to grow at their present rates and that an increase in the rate of growth in America will not influence their rates of economic development. If it turns out that other countries, on their own, pursue policies that accelerate their rates of growth by amounts comparable to the increases that this book assumes will be achieved in the United States, then both the balance of payments and terms of trade effects we have sketched will be far less serious. Adjustment problems would, of course, continue to face us even though foreign incomes were rising faster than they now are, but both the magnitude and general types of difficulties would be comparable to those that will face us if both our and their rates of growth continue as in the recent past.

Even if other countries take no new initiative in fostering more rapid growth, they will be affected by what we do. As we have already argued, our foreign payments will tend to exceed our foreign receipts and this gives a fillip to money incomes abroad. This will induce an increase in their imports, including some from the United States. That, in turn, will remove some of the pressures on our own balance of payments. We have also argued that some of the benefits of more rapid growth in America are likely to accrue to the rest of the world because of changes in the terms of trade, and so real income abroad will rise somewhat more rapidly than the real output of other countries. This rise in real income can be expected to affect favorably the absolute volume of saving abroad and hence to accelerate other countries' rate of growth of real output. If this expansion in productivity and output is matched by pressures to increase money incomes in the same proportion, the results are likely to be favorable to the United States with respect both to the terms of trade and the balance of payments. In sum, this induced expansion abroad may mitigate, in part, some of the previously noted adverse consequences of our expansion.

4. General conclusions. The gist of our conclusions is that, barring a persistent streak of good fortune, an increase in the rate of growth in the United States assumed to be achieved under the proposal advanced here will probably create some balance of payments problems and, in adjusting to these, there will be real costs which will have to be borne out of the increased national income. We have also argued that this cost in real terms will be relatively small, although it might bear very heavily on some sectors.

We fear that the most difficult problems arising out of a sharp improvement in productivity and output relate to the process of making the necessary international monetary adjustments. These financial problems are generally regarded as being transitory in nature, but they *must* be resolved. We are likely to find that a policy of accelerated growth, when other major nations do not follow similar policies, will force us either to raise our import barriers and so to deny ourselves and others some of the benefits of international specialization (the least desirable policy from our point of view), or to pursue internal monetary policies more restrictive than we might advocate if we were a closed economy. Then again, we might be forced to work toward the establishment of new international financial arrangements which would relieve us from serving as the world's foremost international reserve center and thus permit us the freedom, enjoyed by most other countries, of utilizing exchange rate variations as a corrective device.

Our conclusions that we will encounter external economic problems seem on the surface to be at variance with the common belief that countries which grow rapidly seem to do especially well in their international accounts. West Germany and Japan in recent years have frequently been cited as cases in point. Our view of what has happened in those countries is that their favorable external payments position is due not to their higher rate of growth but occurred in spite of it. Their balance of payments position rests on the whole complex of policies they have followed, including not only the receiving, rather than the granting, of much assistance of various kinds from others, but also on a greater ability than many nations have shown to hold the rise in their money incomes more nearly in line with growth of productivity. The experiences of these countries underline the difficulty, in practice, of isolating the effects of economic growth on a nation's external position. They provide specific examples of the statement made in the first paragraph of this chapter to the effect that a nation's international accounts reflect a wide range of economic forces, of which developments surrounding the rate of growth are only a part.

· 9 ·

Some Political Obstacles
to the Implementation
of Economic Growth Proposals

SIDNEY VERBA

Economic growth, as the recent political campaign demonstrated, is widely considered to be an important goal. There are differences as to the urgency of the problem and as to the facts on the current rate of growth in this country and in Russia. But there is relatively little difference as to the importance of the issue. General agreement upon a goal labeled "economic growth," however, does not imply agreement on anything more specific.

The move from agreement upon a general goal to the formulation and implementation of a program to achieve that goal is a difficult move indeed. A general objective such as "economic growth" may receive nearly universal assent. When phrased in such general terms, it appears to be essentially costless and does not conflict with any other aims that individuals or groups may have. Conflicts arise, however, as soon as the specification of a program to achieve the general goal makes apparent the costs of attaining it. The advantage of discussing a specific scheme for accelerating economic growth, as we are doing in this volume, is that it reveals some of the costs, difficulties, and side effects of an attempt to raise the rate of growth. Thus the chapters that deal with the implications of the scheme set forth in Chapter 3 are useful not only as comments on that particular scheme, but also suggest the types of problems one has to consider in dealing with any alternative scheme that has an equally ambitious goal. Similarly, the specification of a scheme for accelerating economic growth facilitates the discussion of the obstacles that may arise to the legislative implementation and successful administration of such a proposal.

This chapter will consider some of the problems inherent in translating a global economic proposal of the kind discussed in this book into an operating legislative program that is capable of achieving the goal the proposal was meant to achieve.

1. Main effects and side effects of a proposal. The members of this group have operated with the following assumptions: (1) an acceleration of the rate of economic growth in the United States is highly desirable, at least for military and diplomatic purposes; (2) such an acceleration will not come of itself, that is, without some action by the government; (3) meaningful changes in the rate of growth can most likely be brought about through some relatively new measures with general impact. The last point raises the difficulties. There are legislative difficulties in changing a continuing program (changing the rates of corporate taxes or the patent laws). But these are mild compared with the problems involved in introducing a totally new program.

A number of specific objections can be raised to the kinds of proposals considered in this book, and later in this chapter we shall consider some of them. First, however, it will be useful to look more generally at the form that such objections might take. In this connection we shall examine the various effects that such proposals can have and the types of objections these effects can engender.

All actions and proposals for action have both main effects and side effects. The main effect of a proposal such as the one discussed in these papers is its impact upon the achievement of the goal it was intended to attain; in this case it is the impact of the proposal on the rate of increase of economic growth. The side effects of a proposal are all other consequences that would flow from its implementation. Thus, many a tax law is instituted in order to raise revenue, and the money raised by it constitutes its main effect. However, it may have side effects upon the distribution of income, the rate of investment, the number of jobs in the government service, and the organization of the government. The side effects of a proposal may be intended or unintended. The designers of a proposal may design it so as to achieve other goals over and above the main objective for which it was designed or to minimize interference with the achievement of other goals. Some intended side effects of the scheme discussed in this book include increased investment and maintenance of a low level of government intervention in the economy. But there are virtually certain to be effects that were not planned by the designers of the proposal. These include unavoidable but expected difficulties as well as unexpected effects. As an example of the former, one can predict that a particular tax measure will lead to an increase in the size of the internal revenue bureau, although this is in no sense a goal of the proposal. An illustration of an unexpected effect might be certain business practices, engendered by the enactment of a proposal, that were neither intended nor predicted by the planners. Lastly, the side effects of a proposal may be good or bad; that is, they may have positive or negative effects on other goals. In connection with this distinction, it is important to note that the main and side effects of a proposal have an impact on many people whose values are different. What may be a negative side effect from one person's point of view may be a positive or neutral side effect from the point of view of another.

These distinctions as to the kinds of effects a proposal such as the one discussed in this book is likely to have are useful in understanding some of the obstacles to its implementation. A specific policy proposal, the impact of which is intended to be general, faces serious obstacles when attempts are made to implement it, even if there is general agreement on the desirability of its goal. The challenges that can be raised against such a proposal derive from its side effects. The proposal will be vulnerable to two types of challenge: general objections based upon a comparison of its costs and its expected accomplishments, and specific challenges directed at the alleviation of some particular side effect.

Even if its consideration is pitched upon a rather high plane, a specific proposal may have disadvantages when compared with other alternatives. One type of alternative is some other proposal that has a main goal roughly similar to that of the one under discussion. The advantage of some alternative proposal under these circumstances is that the nature of the alternative has probably not been as carefully considered as has the current proposal. Hence any negative side effects it might have are likely to be unknown or at least to have less salience. Another type of alternative is the *status quo*. In fact, this is usually the alternative that is in closest competition with a new proposal. The advantages of the *status quo* over the new proposal lie largely in the unexpected side effects of the latter. Whereas the characteristics of the *status quo* are roughly known and have, by definition, been tolerable at least up to the point at which the new proposal is introduced, the new proposal involves uncertainties and may produce anxieties. Such uncertainties may lead to an exaggeration of its undesirable side effects. Moreover, insofar as the new proposal requires change in the bases upon which individuals and firms make their calculations, it also involves specific costs connected with learning to live in a new economic environment. Furthermore, the *status quo* policy requires the least direct effort and, in fact, is the alternative that wins by default, if there is a stalemate over the type of proposal to adopt.

In any case, for a new policy to be chosen over the *status quo,* the undesirable aspects of the *status quo* must be rather clear to those involved in the decision. In this regard, a proposal may create its own obstacles to adoption. Studies of attitude formation show a tendency to adjust one's perceptions and evaluations of a situation in order to maintain a balance between one's goals and one's capabilities. Thus, the specification of the costs of economic growth that accompanies the description of a proposal which is designed for the purpose may lead not only to a decision that economic growth is not worth the effort or the costs, but to a readjustment of one's attitudes toward the desirability of such growth. If it is shown to entail high costs, one may devalue it as a goal. Thus the presentation of a specific proposal may lead not merely to the statement that one does not think the goal is worth the costs but to the belief that one did not really want that goal in the first place.

A more important obstacle to the implementation of a new general economic policy is that it may be discussed, judged, modified, and perhaps accepted or rejected in terms of its side effects alone without any explicit comparison of its main and side effects. There are several reasons for this. The main effect of the kind of general economic policy discussed in this volume is designed to affect a large number and wide range of people. It is, in fact, intended to lead to general changes in the econ-

omy. But the very fact that the main effect is so widely spread
tends to lower the salience of this impact upon any particular
group or individual. In contrast, the side effects of the proposal
often involve only specific groups. Many of these side effects
may be severe and negative as far as these groups are concerned.
Even if the side effect had no greater impact upon the particular group than did the main effect, the very fact that what was
happening to the particular group was not happening to the
general populace, the fact that the group appeared to be sin-
gled out, would lead it to feel resentment toward the proposal.

The strength of the opposition of any group will in turn be
directly related to the intensity of its interest in the proposed
piece of legislation and to the degree of activity it is willing to
undertake. The degree to which any group or individual is
heard during the legislative consideration of a proposed measure is heavily dependent upon the intensity of its interest as
well as its degree of activity. Furthermore, since, as was just
indicated, the opposition is likely to consist, to a considerable
extent, of special groups who expect to suffer from the proposed measure's side effects, a good deal of the discussion of
such a general piece of economic legislation is likely to be
centered on its side effects.

The important point is that the examination of a proposal
is likely to be conducted not in terms of a comparison between
the costs of the side effects and the gains from the main effect,
but rather in terms of the side effects alone. The bulk of Con-
gressional discussion of income tax legislation, for instance,
is not on the costs of achieving its main effect (raising revenue)
but on its side effects (the burdens it places upon particular
groups or types of enterprise).[1] Furthermore, there is evidence

---

[1] For this type of discussion of the Internal Revenue Act of 1954, see
Eugene Neal Feingold, *The Internal Revenue Act of 1954: Policy and
Politics,* unpublished Ph.D. dissertation, Princeton University, 1960.

that members of Congress are likely to consider interest in the proposed legislation that is based on such concrete side effects to be more legitimate (perhaps because it is more understandable) than appeals based on interest in the main effect of the proposal.

This type of challenge to a general economic proposal may be particularly insidious. Those who are injured by a particular side effect may respond not by demanding that the entire program be dropped, but by appealing for relief from that consequence alone. Insofar as the amelioration of any individual side effect does not in itself destroy the program, legislative acquiescence to the request is easy. Thus, relief to the manufacturers of product X does not in itself destroy the main effect and can be dealt with without explicit consideration of the main effect. However, the granting of one exception legitimizes others, and, of course, various groups may join together to support one another's claims. In this way the effectiveness of a program may be destroyed piecemeal. As another consequence, a number of other undesirable side effects, such as inflation or gross inequities, may be accentuated.

This process of erosion through exceptions illustrates the gap that may exist between the criteria used in the formulation of a proposal and the process by which it is judged as it passes through the implementation process. There is likely to be an especially large gap between the (usually quite general) criteria upon which academic economic proposals are based and the criteria used within the legislative process. In a sense this represents the strength as well as the weakness of such academic discussion of policy. Its strength is that it can deal with over-all programs, with the relationship between the main goal of a proposal and its side effects. Its weakness is that by this process it sets up a barrier between proposal and implementation.

2. *Criticisms of the growth proposal.* The task of this chapter is not to estimate the sources of opposition to a measure
of the kind discussed in this volume nor to attempt to predict
its likelihood of success if attempts are made to translate it
into a legislative proposal. Neither shall we try to spell out the
various side effects of the growth proposal nor anticipate the
extent to which they raise objections to the proposal. Many
of the other chapters in this book do this. Our purpose is
merely to suggest that the implementation of any program of
the kind contemplated in this book meets with serious political
obstacles.

The main intended effect of the scheme put forth in this
volume is of course to increase the rate of growth of the
economy of the United States. The most important side effect
of the proposal is to reward certain firms and to penalize
others.[2] In 1960 a group of individuals from business, labor,
and government was asked to comment upon a draft of the
growth proposal. A number of questions were raised by these
individuals as to specific effects the program might have on
inflation, concentration of industries, and the like. These
problems are dealt with elsewhere. Of interest to us here are
the objections raised to the proposal in terms of its main goal
and its main side effect.

Several commentators felt that though accelerated growth
was important, it certainly did not warrant a scheme as "drastic" as that proposed. As might have been expected from our
discussion above, there were suggestions of alternative schemes
as well as suggestions that perhaps the entire problem was
overrated, that accelerated growth was not as vital as our
proposal implied. In particular, comments were made about

---

[2] Though this scheme of rewards and penalties is the most important
aspect of the program, it should be pointed out that the resulting rewards
and punishments are side effects of the program. The goal of the program
is to accelerate rates of growth, not to reward and penalize business firms.

the unexpected consequences of a scheme of this kind, the fact, for instance, that business firms would be motivated to look for unplanned loopholes in the scheme that would mitigate its effect and lead to inequities. As one commentator put it "an old tax is a good tax."

Another type of objection has been raised. This was that the proposal did not deal with other means of accelerating economic growth, in particular with the need for increased government spending on education and research. The objection is interesting in that it was explicitly stated in the proposal that this type of government activity is also important and is in no way in conflict with our own scheme. In fact, we felt that our proposal would be complementary to increased government expenditures in these fields by increasing the revenues available to the Government for these purposes. This suggests another type of obstacle to the implementation of such a proposal. We have seen that vaguely specified alternative proposals may appear attractive when compared with an explicit proposal at hand. Furthermore, it may well be that complementary proposals within the same area will be considered to be in conflict with each other. The very statement that growth can be achieved through a tax rebate scheme may be assumed to be an implicit statement that school construction is unimportant. This is probably a consequence of the fear that the acceptance of any proposal with a particular goal represents per se a denigration of other proposals in the same area.

The most serious obstacle to a proposal of this sort, however, is the possibility that it will be judged in terms of its side effects alone and not in terms of both its main and side effects. The major side effect of this proposal is that it rewards and penalizes individual firms on the basis of their rates of growth. Most of those who commented on the scheme felt that this was in some way unfair, that it might result in windfalls for firms that were expanding through no effort of their own and penalties for firms that could not help the fact that their output was declining somewhat or standing still. Our purpose is not to argue with this criticism. It represents a set of values which have been important in economic policy, as is illustrated by measures to relieve "sick" industries or "sick" areas. Our purpose is to point to the type of objection that is likely to be raised to a growth scheme of the sort we discuss.

The fact that the proposal is designed to avoid giving discretionary power to the Government in its industry by industry application may well increase the possibility that it will be considered in terms of its specific side effects alone. This feature of the proposal means that its effects will fall disproportionately on certain types of firm, in particular, those that may receive windfalls and those that may be penalized. The firms penalized will of course be the center of pressure for exemptions from its provisions. Insofar as these pressures for exemption can be couched in terms of relief for special cases, chronically sick industries, special areas, industries affected by "acts of God," they may very well be accepted without much consideration of the effect of this on the main goal of the scheme. In this connection, the exemptions built into the proposal for administrative and other reasons become particularly important. Each exemption, as was suggested earlier, tends to legitimize others, and the built-in exemptions may open the way for demands that others be accorded similar benefits.

· 10 ·

Concluding Remarks

What then are we to conclude from the discussions presented in this book? Certainly not that the illustrative growth proposal which has served as a focus of its discussion is a panacea for all of our economy's growth problems, or even that, on balance, adoption of the proposal merits the reader's unqualified support. It was not our purpose in writing this book to plead for any specific piece of legislation.

Rather, we feel we have demonstrated the following major points:

(1) It is indeed possible to design policy measures which seem capable of producing a major increase in the rate of growth of our economy *without reliance on direct government controls*. Our illustrative proposal can almost certainly achieve the purpose. By, as it were, tightening the screws sufficiently, by making growth a matter of life and death for the firm and at the same time providing adequate markets for its products and yet keeping inflationary pressure within bounds through standard fiscal policies, there is little doubt that private business could be induced to respond to almost any desired degree. It may well be possible to find alternative and more felicitous courses of action. We maintain only that we have shown in some detail the nature of one policy capable of doing the job. In other words, the situation is by no means hopeless; even if it is true that without greater growth our future is forfeited, we remain masters of our fate.

139

(2) The unpalatability of our illustrative proposal merits re-emphasis. It must involve added hardships for the unsuccessful firm, it will result in substantial administrative costs and problems, particularly because it uses a price deflator in computing value added, and, at least in the beginning, it will require some reduction in the supply of commodities available to consumers. Some difficulties for economic stabilization policy, antitrust policy and the balance of payments are also to be anticipated, though these seem somewhat less likely to be serious.

However, we believe that these and the other social costs which the scheme will incur are simply manifestations of the fact that considerable increases in economic growth cannot be obtained cheaply and easily. The public should not be deluded into thinking otherwise by superficial statements which appear to promise free or at least cut-rate salvation. Any really substantial results will require substantial sacrifices.

(3) We believe that any effective growth program which limits the extent of governmental interference in our economy cannot be very different in structure from our illustrative proposal because if the work is to be carried out by private enterprise, then something must be done to make growth-increasing behavior pay off handsomely to the firm. Furthermore, any such program is likely to have costs very similar to those involved in our plan. We can only challenge the reader who is repelled by this prospect to lay out any specific plan which is very much different, which effectively limits direct Government control and which has any real promise of producing a *substantial* increase in our nation's economic growth. We think he will find that only vague generalities or empty, though stirring, calls to action can be obtained cheaply.

(4) Whether we will want to adopt a growth program, even one which limits Government interference, is a matter of bal-

ancing off costs and advantages. Ultimately, an economic growth program can be considered in the nature of an insurance policy for the western world. And, as in any such decision, the purchaser of the policy should weigh three items: the cost of the policy, the seriousness of the contingency against which the insurance is carried, and the likelihood that this event will occur. It may well be that judicious consideration will lead us to decide that any growth program will cost more than it is worth, but only then will we have come honestly by our complacency in doing little or nothing at all.

However, it is to be emphasized that if doing nothing means that the security of the free world is apt to be slowly but relentlessly undermined then, even if the chances of such an eventuality are not terribly high, the prospect is sufficiently serious to make its prevention worth almost any sacrifices, except, of course, those of giving up the very features of the society which we wish most to preserve. Above all, we must beware of an exchange in which we preserve some comforts today and pay for them with our freedom in the not too distant future. We repeat that if these are indeed the alternatives which really face us, an effective growth program may turn out to be cheap at almost any price.

In any event it is not our function as economists to tell the nation what to set up as its objectives, and we are therefore severely constrained in our policy recommendations. However, if it is indeed true that our economic position relative to that of the Soviet Union is likely to deteriorate in the absence of radical countermeasures, we should not be surprised if there occurs in the future another and more serious repetition of the national fright which accompanied the first sputnik. We would then consider it to be our task to be ready with a carefully conceived program, or perhaps several alternative programs, both in order to facilitate effective policy measures and to make it unnecessary for the nation to turn to the political quacks, the demagogues, and the unscrupulous individuals whom history has shown to be all too ready to take advantage of desperation and panic. It is in this spirit, the desire to have explored the requisites of an effective program and its costs, that this study has been undertaken.

· *APPENDIX A* ·

The Appropriate Rate
of Growth
of National Output

WILLIAM J. BAUMOL

1. National output and the resources available to the public sector. It has been the basic point of view of this book that economic growth is desired not primarily for its own sake, but rather as a means for inducing the economy to make more resources available to the public sector for use in programs such as research, education, aid to underdeveloped areas, and military preparation. In practice, a government's freedom to change the allocation of the nation's resources is usually highly restricted. It is notorious that few political systems are able to impose on their citizens anything like the drastic savings rates which the Soviets have been able to achieve. Equally noteworthy is the fact that none of the rather prosperous western European nations has been able to afford to keep up with the United States and the Soviet Union in the race for prestige and power. It was simply impossible, politically, for them to draw enough income away from the private sector.

Since in a democratic country it is difficult to increase very substantially the government's slice of the pie at the expense of the private sector, it becomes expedient to obtain a larger pie so that both sectors can increase their consumption together. This is one of the main reasons behind our concern with the growth of national output as an instrument of foreign policy.

We shall see now that this observation permits us to construct models and make calculations about the rates of growth in income required to achieve specific targets for the activities of the public sector. Specifically, we shall now seek to answer the following question. Suppose a growth scheme such as that described in this book has been put into operation, and it is found that by varying tax and rebate rates, any of a considerable range of rates of growth of national income, Y, can be attained. Given some target rate of growth of government outlay, G, which is dictated by considerations of national policy, what is an appropriate rate of growth in national income? That is, what rate of growth in Y will provide the public sector with the desired quantity of resources?

2. Calculation of a required rate of growth. Let us for the moment ignore the dependence of the expenditure decisions of the private sector on the Government's monetary and fiscal arrangements, except for the stimulating effects of government outlays which occur through the multiplier process. The critical role of saving in any growth program, as a source of resources both for investment by the private sector and for use by the Government, has been emphasized at several points in this book. Accordingly, my basic premise in this appendix is that, in our economy, the Government can, without political or economic strain, take for itself only that portion of output which represents voluntary saving by the private sector, purchasing power which the public does not desire to spend on consumer or producer goods. This at once yields a trivial equation which tells us how national income must change in order to permit the achievement of any specific target rate of growth in public spending. We have[1]

(1) $$Y = E + G$$

where, again, Y represents the requisite level of total national output and E and G symbolize desired private and governmental expenditures respectively. Assuming, to begin with, that desired private outlays are dependent only on *current* income we may write $E = f(Y)$. Substituting this expression into Equation (1) and differentiating with respect to G we obtain

$$\frac{dY}{dG} = f' \frac{dY}{dG} + 1$$

or (2) $$\frac{dY}{dG} = \frac{1}{1 - f'}$$

This equation looks very much like the usual multiplier relationship, since f' is the marginal propensity to spend (consume) by the private sector, $1 - f'$ is its marginal propensity to save and its reciprocal, $1/1 - f'$, is the garden variety multiplier. However, Equation (2) is the usual multiplier relationship as it were, stood up on its head. Rather than indicating what rise in income, dY, will result from a given rise in government outlay, dG, we have sought to determine *the magnitude of the rise in income necessary to release the resources, dG, for use by the public sector.*[2] We have thus arrived at the rather obvious

---

[1] This is obviously a standard and highly simple multiplier model. The reader may also observe that it is a trivial input-output model, one in which the entire economy has been aggregated into a single sector. Here G may be interpreted as a target final output, and E as that portion of Y which must be used up as an intermediate step in order to make G available. As is usual in an input-output analysis, the model asks how much total output, Y, must be produced in order for us to end up with the target net output, G.

[2] Equation (2) then may be interpreted as giving us the *required* rate

result that if the multiplier is, for example, 3, then an X dollar increase in public expenditure which is to be taken out of voluntary private savings must be accompanied by a $3X$ dollar rise in national income.

Let us carry the argument one step further. Rates of growth are customarily and conveniently expressed in percentage terms. Hence, it is appropriate to examine how a given percentage change in Government expenditure, $100 \ G'/G$, affects the percentage change in national income, $100 \ Y'/Y$, necessary to produce the requisite voluntary savings. The resulting expression, which may conveniently be called the required income-government outlay growth ratio,[3] can be written with the aid of Equation (2) as

$$(3) \qquad \frac{Y'/Y}{G'/G} = \frac{dY}{dG}\frac{G}{Y} = \frac{1}{1-f'}\frac{G}{Y}$$

Now, G/Y, the proportion of current Government outlay to national income, is a known figure. For the moment, for example, we may take it to be about 0.2. Hence, we can see from our last equation that a Z per cent rise in Government outlay will also call for a Z per cent rise in national output if and only if the marginal propensity to save (on the part of business and consumers together), $1 - f'$, is 20 per cent as well. In fact, we can construct a simple table showing the relationship between the value of the propensity to save and the required income-government outlay growth ratio:

marginal propensity to save $(1-f')$	0.05	0.1	0.15	0.2	0.25	0.3
$\dfrac{dY}{dG}\dfrac{G}{Y}\left(=0.2\dfrac{1}{1-f'}\right)$	4	2	1.33	1	0.8	0.67

of growth of national income, that is (if one may borrow the term), the rate of growth of income warranted by the needs of the public sector. If, in fact, the public sector spends the amount G, total effective demand, E plus G, will be equal to the quantity of output so that Equation (2) will also yield the *equilibrium* time path of output.

[3] For obvious reasons it is also tempting to call it something like "the Government outlay elasticity of national income."

This table tells us that if the private sector's marginal propensity to save is less than 20 per cent, a given percentage rise in Government expenditure will require a more than proportionate rise in national income. In other words, as Government expenditures increase they must nevertheless constitute an ever declining proportion of the national product. For example, if the marginal propensity to save is 0.1, a 3 per cent rise in Government expenditure must be accompanied by twice as large a rise in national income (6 per cent)! In contrast, if the marginal propensity to save exceeds 0.2, national income does not have to be raised quite in proportion with governmental outlay, and the share of the public sector in the economy will grow with rises in government expenditure.

The logic of these results is really very simple. It amounts to the view that if Government expenditures are to be taken out of voluntary savings, then the smaller the propensity to save, the greater must be the income stimulus needed to induce the public to supply the Government with a given level of real resources.

3. *The role of fiscal policy.* The preceding analysis clearly does not take sufficient account of the Government's power to influence the course of events. Obviously, if people do not voluntarily save as much as the state wants to use for public purposes, it can force its citizens to save more by taxing purchasing power away from them. It is hardly necessary to point out that there are limits to the extent to which a country can increase taxation without creating serious problems of incentive distortion, morale and political opposition. However, the magnitudes of these limits, even if they can meaningfully be defined and discovered, are largely beside the point. An important objective of a growth program for national output would be to avoid any necessity of approaching these limits, to smooth the path of the Government in achieving its expenditure goals. Where resources cannot readily be forced out of the hands of the people, they must be induced to save more by sufficient increases in real income.

Nevertheless, fiscal policy does offer greater flexibility to the Government than the model of the preceding section suggests. An increase in taxes may be taken primarily as a device for decreasing the marginal propensity to consume out of income (before taxes). Expression (3), as well as common sense, tells us that this will reduce the magnitude of the rise in national income needed to achieve a given Government expenditure growth program. Thus the policy maker can choose between higher taxes or faster economic growth as a means for financing increased public outlays, and perhaps he will want to employ some combination of the two for this purpose.

It may be noted, however, that consideration of long-run political goals rather than short-run expediency may well recommend caution in the use of taxation for this purpose. First of all, there are the much discussed discouraging effects of taxation on incentives, and it is clear that an excessive increase in taxes may have seriously damaging effects on the performance of the economy. There is also a second, somewhat less obvious reason for going slowly on tax increases. For as Equation (3) indicates, a sufficiently small propensity to consume can lead to a required income-government outlay growth ratio $[(dY/dG) \times (G/Y)]$ which is less than unity. This means that real income will rise less than proportionately with government outlay, and the role of the public sector will therefore increase in importance. We may well be concerned if this excess in the rate of expansion of governmental over private incomes is substantial and protracted. It may therefore be worth considering the rather radical suggestion that, over the long run, fiscal policy be used to support the propensity to consume as a means for limiting the role of the public sector, even during the course of expansion programs designed to provide more resources for governmental use.

Of course, an optimal tax level-growth rate policy combination must involve a balancing off of social costs and advantages. Thus, whereas moderate tax levels mean, on the one hand, that the share of the public sector can remain relatively small they will, on the other hand, require a much larger rate of growth of national output, with all its attendant social costs, in order to permit the attainment of a given target of resource availability for the public sector.

At any rate these observations suggest that a different strategy is required of functional finance when growth in the level of public expenditure becomes an important proximate goal and unemployment and inflation are not the most critical economic problems facing the economy.

4. Geometry of the analysis. In Figure 1 we have the conventional 45° diagram representing the determination of national income. The line SS' is the private sector's propensity to spend curve. Since residual (unspent) output is taken to be used by the Government, the outlay of the public sector at any income level is indicated by the vertical distance between SS' and the 45° line (the total income line). For example, at income level Y_0 we see that $G_0 = AB$ will be available to the Government.

Now in Figure 1a, where SS' is a straight line through the origin, it is clear that governmental resources and national income will rise strictly in proportion; G_1 will be twice the length of G_0 if and only if income Y_1 is twice as large as Y_0. A proof by similar triangles is quite obvious. In the same way, in Figure 1b we see that where SS' is less steep than a straight line through the origin, governmental expenditure can be

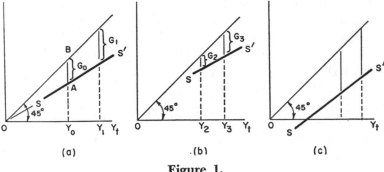

Figure 1.

increased more than in proportion to national income; the doubling of public sector outlay from G_2 to G_3 requires a much smaller proportionate rise in income from Y_2 to Y_3. Similarly, Figure 1c illustrates that a declining share of Government outlay in a growing economy results from a propensity to spend curve whose slope is steeper than that of a straight line through the origin.[4]

Now let us see what happens if the marginal propensity to spend curve is nonlinear. First let us examine the case where it grows steadily flatter as we move toward the right (monotonically diminishing marginal propensity to spend), as in Figure 2a. Suppose that there is some point P on SS' at which its slope is greater than that of a straight line through the

---

[4] We may note that this is no more than a geometric version of our results in Section 3. For the slope (the private sector's marginal propensity to spend, *MPE*) of a straight SS' line through the *origin* like that in Figure 1a is always equal to E/Y (where E, as before, represents total private expenditure). But since Government spending, G, equals $Y - E$, we have

$$MPE = E/Y = (Y - G)/Y = 1 - G/Y \quad \text{or} \quad 1 - MPE = G/Y$$

This is the same as the result which follows from Equation (3)—if public and total outlays are to grow in proportion, as they do in Figure 1a, we must have the private sector's marginal propensity to save equal to G/Y. Figures 1b and 1c may be interpreted similarly.

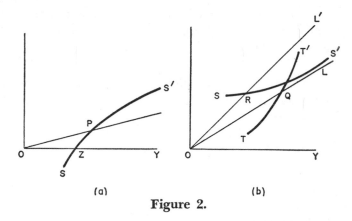

Figure 2.

origin. Then *SS'* must cut the horizontal axis somewhere to the right of the origin (point *Z*). This means that below some positive level of income, *OZ*, private spending will be zero or negative, an assertion which under normal economic circumstances is rather implausible. We may take it, then, that a diminishing marginal propensity to spend curve will generally rise less steeply than a straight line through the origin.[5] It follows that a diminishing marginal private propensity to spend generally makes it easier for the Government to acquire increased resources (less of an increase in income is needed to get the public to save the required amount) and that, as a corollary, such a relationship will tend to result in an increase in the share of the public sector as output and public expenditure grow. In particular, it may be suspected that progressive

---

[5] Unfortunately, as Figure 2b indicates, no analogous argument can be used in the case of an increasing marginal propensity to spend. *SS'* in that diagram is asymptotic to *OL* and at any point such as *R*, its slope is less than that of a straight line through the origin. But propensity to spend curve *TT'* also involves an increasing marginal propensity to spend, and is steeper than *OL* at *Q*. Thus an increasing marginal propensity to spend curve can, apparently, be either more or less steep than a straight line through the origin.

taxation will have such an effect since it tends to reduce the share of private expenditure out of pre-tax income as the income level rises.

5. A dynamic model. To investigate the long-run prospects and the stability properties of an economy with a steadily growing government outlay it is necessary to construct a dynamic model. The number of possible models is very large indeed, and the appropriate model is an empirical matter which I am in no position to judge. I therefore present only a very simple prototype involving just a minor departure from Equation (1). Employing the usual lagged relationship for the propensity to spend we obtain (using E, K, and R as constants)

$$Y_t = EY_{t-1} + G_t + K$$
$$G_t = RG_{t-1}$$

where $R > 1$ is the desired rate of growth of government expenditure, and the private expenditure function is $EY_{t-1} + K$, where presumably $0 < E < 1$. This pair of first order linear difference equations can easily be shown to have the solution

$$Y_t = \frac{G_0}{R - E} R^{t+1} + bE^{t+1} + \frac{K}{1 - E}$$
$$G_t = G_0 R^t$$

where G_0 is the initial level of government outlay and b is a constant whose value is dependent on both Y_0 and G_0.

Since $0 < E < 1$, the second term in the expression for Y_t will eventually become negligible. Moreover, since $R > 1$ the first term will grow without limit, and relatively speaking, the last term will become insignificant. The ratio of Y_t to G_t will then asymptotically approach the positive constant $R/(R - E)$. Thus, in the linear case, we may expect that the ratio

$$\frac{Y_t}{G_t} = \frac{R}{R - E} + b\frac{E}{G_0}\left(\frac{E}{R}\right)^t + \frac{K}{G_0(1 - E)}\left(\frac{1}{R}\right)^t$$

will fall perpetually but not without limit. The economic implication is that the public sector will grow relative to the private sector, but this expansion will be bounded and will never go beyond the point where the ratio between governmental and private expenditure falls to $(R - E)/R = 1 - E/R$. That is, the minimal ratio of private to total expenditure will be E/R. As an illustrative order of magnitude, suppose an income expansion program permits government expenditure to grow at 10 per cent per annum so that $R = 1.1$, and the marginal private propensity to spend for both consumption and investment, E, is 0.8. Then the share of the private sector will never fall below 72 per cent of the national output!

6. Conclusion. This appendix has presented several highly simplified and rather artificial models designed to exhibit the relationship between any desired rate of expansion of governmental expenditure and the rate of expansion of national income necessary to make these resources available to the Government. The shortcomings of the models should not be permitted to obscure two essential conclusions: first, that in a democratic society the government cannot obtain all the resources it needs just by fiat, and that, therefore, a program of general economic expansion may be necessary as a means to obtain these resources, and second, that such a combined growth program is by no means tantamount to the abandonment of the system of private enterprise for it does not necessarily involve a substantial increase in the role of the public sector of the economy.

· *APPENDIX B* ·

Effects of the Tax-Subsidy Plan:
Some Theoretical Analyses

RICHARD E. QUANDT

1. Calculation of real value added. The calculation of "real" or "constant dollar" quantities is usually accomplished by deflating current dollar figures with an appropriate price index. This task becomes considerably more complicated when the quantity to be deflated is value added. Assume for simplicity that inventory levels are constant and thus sales equal production.[1] Denoting the current value of sales by S and the current value of the cost of materials purchased by M, the gross value added is $S - M$. There is no "natural" price index for this quantity. It would surely be inappropriate to use a price index of items sold (denoted by p_s) for deflating $S - M$. It would be equally inappropriate to use a price index of materials' cost p_m for this purpose. In fact, in order to get a quasi-physical measure of value added, the quantities S and M must be separately converted into physical units by deflating each by its appropriate price index. The difference between the two quantities, S/p_s and M/p_m, is then a measure of real gross value added.

A recent attempt to measure real value added by industrial

---

[1] The assumption that sales equal production is made for convenience here and elsewhere in this section but is not necessary for the arguments advanced.

origin avoids some of the difficulties inherent in the formulation above but only at the cost of an implicit assumption of questionable validity.[2] The authors' objective was to construct indices of value added price[3] for the various industries. Their method employed the following steps:

"1. For each major industry, a series on gross income originating was constructed. . . .

2. An index of *real output* was constructed for each major industry. . . .

3. Constant dollar gross product in each industry was estimated by multiplying the base year gross income originating by the output index." [4] Denote the current dollar value of sales and materials in two periods by

$$S_0, S_1, M_0, M_1 \quad \text{and let their prices be} \quad p_{s_0}, p_{s_1}, p_{m_0}, p_{m_1}$$

(As before, inventory change is disregarded.) Then real gross value added in period 1 (period 1 value added in terms of period 0 dollars) is

$$(1) \qquad (S_0 - M_0)\left(\frac{S_1/p_{s_1}}{S_0/p_{s_0}}\right)$$

where the second parenthesis is the output index. It is clear from the preceding argument that the proper formulation is

$$(2) \qquad (S_0 - M_0)\left(\frac{S_1/p_{s_1} - M_1/p_{m_1}}{S_0/p_{s_0} - M_0/p_{m_0}}\right)$$

where the second parenthesis is an index of real value added. A necessary condition for the equality of the two measures can

---

[2] C. L. Schultze, *Prices, Costs and Output for the Post War Decade: 1947-1957* (Committee for Economic Development); C. L. Schultze and J. L. Tryon, *Prices and Costs in Manufacturing Industries* (Joint Economic Committee, Study Paper No. 17, January 25, 1960).

[3] A value added price is one which converts dollar figures of value added into physical equivalents upon dividing it into the dollar amounts.

[4] C. L. Schultze, *op. cit.*, pp. 15-16. My italics.

be derived by setting Equation (1) equal to Equation (2). Simplifying the resulting expression one obtains

(3) $$\frac{S_1/p_{s_1}}{S_0/p_{s_0}} = \frac{M_1/p_{m_1}}{M_0/p_{m_0}}$$

which is the implicit assumption underlying the Schultze-Tryon formulation. In effect the assumption says that the physical measure of materials purchased has moved in the same proportion as the physical measure of sales.[5] Whether this assumption is true or not is, of course, an empirical proposition which can hardly be judged on a priori grounds. It would be a considerable advantage to find independent evidence that the assumption is reasonable since the Schultze-Tryon formulation does not appear to require a price index of materials purchased.[6]

2. A partial equilibrium approach: the value added model.

This and the following section consider the effect on an indi-

---

[5] The employment of value added weights in the production indices utilized in the Schultze-Tryon formulation follows the precedent of the Federal Reserve Board indices of industrial production. (See Schultze and Tryon, *op. cit.*, p. 8 and footnote and also *Industrial Production 1959 Revision*, Board of Governors of the Federal Reserve System, Washington, D.C., 1960, pp. 26-41.) The latter publication states (p. 36) that "The industrial production index is an approximation to a measure of value added in the constant prices of the weight period." Nevertheless, the weighting by value added weights does not convert the production index into a value added index. The former is an approximation to the latter only to the extent that the assumption expressed in Equation (3) is approximately fulfilled.

[6] The assumption is made explicitly by J. Alterman and Eva E. Jacobs, "Estimates of Real Product in the United States by Industrial Sector, 1947-55," *Studies in Income and Wealth*, Vol. 25 (National Bureau of Economic Research), forthcoming. Whether the assumption is a good one for the period 1947-55 cannot be tested, of course, by reference to figures calculated on the basis of the assumption. In any case, the method proposed by Alterman and Jacobs and adopted by Schultze can only be considered an imperfect long-run substitute for the proper measure required.

vidual firm of two related growth schemes of the type discussed in this book. The analysis is in terms of elementary theoretical models showing the consequences of stimulating growth both by the value added approach and the sales approach. Both models necessarily abstract from numerous details of reality. Nevertheless, they have the property that they lead to propositions which are at least conceivably testable, that is, which can at least conceivably be falsified by reference to data. The models are merely two of a whole family of related theoretical formulations. Actual implementation of these models is, of course, impossible without data generated through the operation of the scheme.

The value-added model and the sales model (to be described subsequently) have one feature in common, namely, that the price of the product and the prices of materials purchased and factors hired are assumed to be given parameters. This means that the firm is regarded as a pure competitor in input and product markets and that the price level is not affected by exogenous factors such as the level of aggregate spending. Although these assumptions are fairly restrictive, they are helpful in permitting one to concentrate on certain other essential features of the problem. As before, inventory change is neglected, that is, it is assumed that production equals sales.

Measuring quantities in terms of dollars, define the variables and parameters of the problem as follows:

S = quantity of product sold
M = quantity of materials purchased
F = quantity of factors (labor and capital) hired
Y = net income
c = corporate income tax rate
k = penalty tax rate
a = rebate rate coefficient
S_0, M_0 = initial (last year's) values of sales and materials
T = total tax minus rebate

We then have the following relationships:

the production function, $f(M, F) = S$

$$S - M = \text{value added}$$

$$S - M - F = Y \quad \text{(net operating income)}$$

$$\frac{S - M - S_0 + M_0}{S_0 - M_0} = \text{growth rate}$$

$$a \frac{(S - M - S_0 + M_0)}{S_0 - M_0} = \begin{array}{l}\text{effective rebate rate (being}\\ \text{a linear function of the rate}\\ \text{of growth)}\end{array}$$

$$a \frac{(S - M - S_0 + M_0)(S - M)}{S_0 - M_0} = \text{total rebate.}$$

Therefore

$$T = cY + k(S - M) - a \frac{(S - M)^2}{S_0 - M_0} + a(S - M)$$

and net profit after taxes and rebate

$$(4) \quad \Pi = (1 - c - k - a)(S - M) - (1 - c)F + a \frac{(S - M)^2}{S_0 - M_0}$$

It is assumed that firms maximize net profits after taxes and rebate. The maximization of the profit function, Equation 4, is accomplished mathematically as follows:

Substituting $f(M, F)$ for S in (4) and setting the first partial derivatives equal to zero,

$$(5) \quad \frac{\partial \Pi}{\partial M} = (1 - c - k - a)(f_1 - 1) + \frac{2a(f - M)(f_1 - 1)}{S_0 - M_0} = 0$$

$$(6) \quad \frac{\partial \Pi}{\partial F} = (1 - c - k - a)f_2 - (1 - c) + \frac{2a(f - M)f_2}{S_0 - M_0} = 0$$

where $\partial f / \partial M = f_1$ and $\partial f / \partial F = f_2$. Writing A for $1 - c - k - a$ and B for $2a/(S_0 - M_0)$, both constants, we have

$$(7) \qquad A(f_1 - 1) + B(f - M)(f_1 - 1) = 0$$

$$(8) \qquad Af_2 - (1 - c) + B(f - M)f_2 = 0$$

These equations imply

(9) $$f_1 = 1$$

(10) $$f_2 = \frac{1 - c}{A + 2a(1 + G)}$$

where G is the percentage rate of growth.

It may be objected that Equation (7) possesses a solution if $f_1 \neq 1$. In that case, however, $1 - c - k + a = -2aG$ which is implausible in the light of the values assigned to the parameters in Chapters 3 and 4. According to the schedule in Chapter 3, $k = .01$, and $a = .2$. In addition, the value of c can be assumed to be .5. $f_1 \neq 1$ would then imply a rate of growth of minus 172.5 per cent. It follows further that for virtually all plausible values of c, k, a, and G that $f_2 < 1$.

Clearly this is reasonable; materials will be bought up to the point where a marginal dollar spent on materials brings in exactly one extra dollar of revenue and factors will be hired beyond that point. Since, without a growth plan, all inputs would be bought only up to the point where their price equalled their marginal revenue product, output in this case will be greater than without a growth plan.

The second partial derivatives are (utilizing $f_1 - 1 = 0$)

$$\frac{\partial^2 \Pi}{\partial M^2} = [A + B(f - M)]f_{11} = r_{11}$$

$$\frac{\partial^2 \Pi}{\partial F^2} = [A + B(f - M)]f_{22} + Bf_2{}^2 = r_{22}$$

$$\frac{\partial^2 \Pi}{\partial M \partial F} = [A + B(f - M)]f_{12} = r_{12}$$

Second order conditions for a maximum are

$$r_{11} < 0, \quad r_{22} < 0, \quad \begin{vmatrix} r_{11} & r_{12} \\ r_{12} & r_{22} \end{vmatrix} > 0$$

Since $A + B(f - M)$ is positive for plausible values of the parameters, the second order conditions $r_{11} < 0$, $r_{22} < 0$ imply that $f_{11} < 0$ and $f_{22} < 0$. We further observe that the sign of r_{12} will be the same as that of f_{12}. It will be assumed that f_{12} is non-negative, that is, that the marginal product of materials is nondiminishing as the quantity of labor and other factors is increased.

In order to find the effect of a change in a parameter on M and F we take the total differentials of Equations (7) and (8).

If a is allowed to change we have to solve

$$\begin{bmatrix} r_{11} & r_{12} \\ r_{12} & r_{22} \end{bmatrix} \begin{bmatrix} dM \\ dF \end{bmatrix} = \begin{bmatrix} 0 \\ f_2[1 - 2(1 + G)]da \end{bmatrix}$$

or, denoting $r_{11}r_{22} - r_{12}^2$ by Δ,

$$\frac{dM}{da} = -\frac{r_{12}f_2[1 - 2(1 + G)]}{\Delta}$$

$$\frac{dF}{da} = \frac{r_{11}f_2[1 - 2(1 + G)]}{\Delta}$$

For plausible ranges of parameters dF/da is positive and dM/da non-negative. Thus, with a rate of growth higher than minus 50 per cent, the quantity $[1 - 2(1 + G)]$ is negative. Since the marginal product f_2 is positive and r_{11} negative, dF/da is positive. If both F and M increase with a, so does output.

When c varies, the analogus procedure gives

$$\frac{dM}{dc} = \frac{-r_{12}(f_2 - 1)}{\Delta} \geqq 0$$

$$\frac{dF}{dc} = \frac{r_{11}(f_2 - 1)}{\Delta} > 0$$

where the signs of the derivatives are obtained by recalling that $f_2 < 1$.

When k varies:

$$\frac{dM}{dk} = \frac{-r_{12}f_2}{\Delta} \leqq 0$$

$$\frac{dF}{dk} = \frac{r_{11}f_2}{\Delta} < 0$$

Defining the elasticity e_{Mk} as $\left|\frac{dM}{dk}\frac{k}{M}\right|$ and all other elasticities analogously, we have

$$e_{Mk} = \frac{r_{12}f_2k}{M\Delta} \qquad\qquad e_{Fk} = \frac{-r_{11}f_2k}{F\Delta}$$

$$e_{Ma} = \frac{-r_{12}[1 - 2(1 + G)]f_2a}{M\Delta} \qquad e_{Fa} = \frac{r_{11}[1 - 2(1 + G)]f_2a}{F\Delta}$$

$$e_{Mc} = \frac{-r_{12}(f_2 - 1)c}{M\Delta} \qquad\qquad e_{Fc} = \frac{r_{11}(f_2 - 1)c}{F\Delta}$$

Making the plausible assumption that[7]

$$k < -[1 - 2(1 + G)]a$$

we have

$$e_{Ma} > e_{Mk}$$

$$e_{Fa} > e_{Fk}$$

The following conclusions then follow from the assumption of profit maximization:

(1) An increase in the rebate rate coefficient a will increase both factors and materials purchased and will thus increase output.

(2) At the maximum Π output will be greater than without the growth plan.

---

[7] Asserting the opposite, $\frac{1}{2}(k/a - 1) \geqq G$. For values of k and a anywhere near those assumed for illustrative purposes, the rate of growth would have to be significantly negative to satisfy the inequality in this footnote. The reader may verify that this is even more implausible if the scheme is self-liquidating (see Section 3) in which case $k = aG$.

(3) An increase in the penalty tax rate k will diminish output.

(4) An increase in the corporate tax rate c will *increase* output in the presence of the growth plan (!).

(5) Moreover, as we have just seen,

$$e_{Mk} < e_{Ma}$$

$$e_{Fk} < e_{Fa}$$

for certain reasonable ranges of growth rates and tax-rebate schedules.[8]

Conclusions (1), (2) and (3) are clearly what one would expect. On a theoretical level they indicate that the growth plan under consideration would tend to provide the right kind of incentive. Conclusion (4) is somewhat paradoxical and has to be investigated further. Only an intuitive argument will be given in explanation of this proposition.

Consider a situation in which the firm has attained an equilibrium position, given the corporate and penalty tax rates and given the rebate rate coefficient. This position of equilibrium is characterized by the entrepreneur's indifference between maintaining the corresponding output level or increasing it by an infinitesimal amount. If he increased his output, his rate of growth of value added would increase, and so would his receipts on the rebate account. Since he is already producing beyond the output level which is optimal in the complete absence of a growth plan, an increase in output would diminish profits from his operations. On the margin, these two changes will just cancel. If, now, the corporate income tax rate were raised, the entrepreneur would keep a smaller percentage of the marginal profit dollar; hence, if before the change in c he was just indifferent between raising his output

---

[8] Additional relationships among the various elasticities can be discovered by making specific assumptions about the values of the parameters.

by one unit or not, it will now pay him to do so. An increase in output will still raise his rebate receipts as before but will diminish his net profit from operations by less than before.

An additional conclusion can be extracted from the model. It has been seen that the incentive to produce an output which is larger than the output that would have been produced in the absence of the growth scheme is provided by the fact that the diminution in operating profit due to a larger than optimal output is more than compensated for by subsidy payments. It then follows that the extent to which a firm is stimulated depends upon how fast operating profits decline when output is pushed beyond the optimal level. But the rate of decline of operating profits is governed by the rate of decline of the marginal product of factors and materials. If some of these marginal products become very low as capacity output is approached and if technical substitutability of inputs is generally low, the growth scheme will not provide much incentive to raise output.

3. The sales model. An alternative formulation of the growth proposal involves rebate payments the rate of which depends upon the rate of growth in sales (or production). In this case both the penalty tax rate and the rebate rate are applied to dollar sales as a base. In that case the profit function to be maximized and analogous to Equation (4) is

$$(11) \qquad \Pi = (1 - c)(S - M - F) - kS + a\frac{S^2}{S_0} - aS$$

Substituting $f(M, F)$ for S in Equation (11) and setting the first partial derivatives equal to zero,

$$(12) \qquad \frac{\partial \Pi}{\partial M} = (1 - c - k - a)f_1 - (1 - c) + \frac{2af(M, F)f_1}{S_0} = 0$$

$$(13) \qquad \frac{\partial \Pi}{\partial F} = (1 - c - k - a)f_2 - (1 - c) + \frac{2af(M, F)f_2}{S_0} = 0$$

One immediately infers that $f_1 = f_2$. This result differs from the corresponding result in Section B-2 [see Equations (9) and (10)], for clearly the value added approach discriminates against material purchases and thus relatively more factors will be bought in that case than in the present one. Since Equations (12) and (13) imply

$$f_1 \left[1 - c - k - a + \frac{2af(M, F)}{S_0} \right] = 1 - c$$

$$f_2 \left[1 - c - k - a + \frac{2af(M, F)}{S_0} \right] = 1 - c$$

we can infer that the stated values of the parameters result in marginal productivities f_1 and f_2 less than unity (unless the rate of growth of sales G is of the order of about $-.5$).[9] The results concerning marginal products can thus be summarized as follows:

No Growth Plan	Value Added Plan	Sales Plan
$f_1 = 1$	$f_1 = 1$	$f_1 < 1$
$f_2 = 1$	$f_2 < 1$	$f_2 < 1$

Assuming, as before, that $f_{12} \geqq 0$, the lowest output is achieved without the growth scheme. With diminishing marginal product, both value added and sales plans result in higher employment of factors or materials and thus lead to higher output.

Proceeding as we did in Section 2, we obtain

$$\frac{dM}{da} = \frac{f_1[1 - 2(1 + G)]r_{22} - f_2[1 - 2(1 + G)]r_{12}}{\Delta} > 0$$

$$\frac{dF}{da} = \frac{-f_1[1 - 2(1 + G)]r_{12} + f_2[1 - 2(1 + G)]r_{11}}{\Delta} > 0$$

$$\frac{dM}{dc} = \frac{-r_{22}(1 - f_1) + r_{12}(1 - f_2)}{\Delta} > 0$$

[9] Assume, for example, that sales remained constant. Given $c = .5$, $k = .01$, $a = .2$, $f_1 = f_2 \cong .46$.

$$\frac{dF}{dc} = \frac{r_{12}(1 - f_1) - r_{11}(1 - f_2)}{\Delta} > 0$$

$$\frac{dM}{dk} = \frac{r_{22}f_1 - r_{12}f_2}{\Delta} < 0$$

$$\frac{dF}{dk} = \frac{-r_{12}f_1 + r_{11}f_2}{\Delta} < 0$$

where r_{11}, r_{12}, r_{22} are the second partial derivatives of Equation (11), and Δ is $r_{11}r_{22} - r_{12}{}^2$. As before, second order conditions for a maximum require $r_{11} < 0$, $r_{22} < 0$, $\Delta > 0$.

The signs of the derivatives can be ascertained by recalling the second order conditions and the fact that $f_1 < 1$, $f_2 < 1$. One also has to assume that $r_{12} \gtreqless 0$ which follows (by a plausibility argument) from the assumption that $f_{12} \gtreqless 0$ and the definition

$$\frac{\partial^2 \Pi}{\partial M \partial F} \equiv r_{12} = f_{12}[1 - c - k - a + 2a(1 + G)]$$

Thus changes in the values of the parameters affect the variables in the same manner qualitatively as in the value added approach.

Finally, the relevant elasticities (in absolute value terms) are

$$e_{Mk} = -\frac{k(r_{22}f_1 - r_{12}f_2)}{M\Delta}$$

$$e_{Fk} = -\frac{k(r_{11}f_2 - r_{12}f_1)}{F\Delta}$$

$$e_{Ma} = \frac{a[1 - 2(1 + G)](r_{22}f_1 - r_{12}f_2)}{M\Delta}$$

$$e_{Fa} = \frac{a[1 - 2(1 + G)](r_{11}f_2 - r_{12}f_1)}{F\Delta}$$

whence a plausibility argument similar to the previous ones results in

$$e_{Ma} > e_{Mk}$$

$$e_{Fa} > e_{Fk}$$

The conclusions emerging from the analysis are:

(1) An increase in the rebate rate coefficient a will increase both factors and materials purchased and will thus increase output.

(2) For reasonable values of the parameters (see Section 2) output will be greater than without the growth plan.

(3) An increase in the penalty tax rate k will diminish output.

(4) An increase in the corporate tax rate c will increase output in the presence of the growth plan.

(5) $e_{Ma} > e_{Mk}$

$e_{Fa} > e_{Fk}$

The conclusions are almost identical with those reached in the value added approach. Finally, one can also show that if identical values were assigned to the parameters in the value added and sales approaches, the latter would lead to a higher output if, at the relevant range of operations, an increase in sales could be accomplished only with a more than proportionate increase in raw material purchases.

Conclusion (4) is the same, somewhat paradoxical result encountered in the value added case. The validity of this conclusion can be ascertained intuitively with an argument analogous to that employed in the value added case.

4. Towards some econometric models. If a growth plan of the type described in this book were actually to be introduced, one would have to decide upon some particular rate structure. One would presumably require that the specified penalty tax and rebate rates be effective, yet be moderate enough to avoid sudden and violent dislocations in the economy. One might further wish to require that, if the economy achieved the target rate of growth, the plan be self-liquidating, that is, that the penalty taxes collected be just sufficient to pay the aggregate rebates. Decisions concerning tax rates and rebate rates will clearly have to depend on the effectiveness of such a growth plan. It is therefore necessary to provide a method by which the effectiveness of the plan could be measured.

A simple model. Two basic relationships are at work in the simplest formulation. The Government observes the growth rates of each firm and makes certain rebate payments to them. At the same time, firms observe the rebate payments and adjust their rate of growth.

Strictly speaking, the observed growth rate of a firm does not determine its receipts on rebate account but merely the rebate *rate.* Conversely, it is not implausible to argue that the firm will base its decisions to alter the rate of growth on the rebate rate achieved rather than on the actual rebate payments to it. The mathematical expression for the Government's rebate rate function is

(14) $$R = aG$$

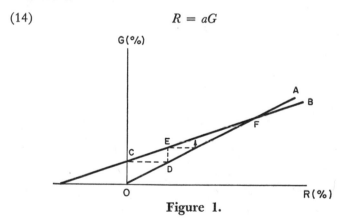

Figure 1.

where R is the rebate rate (applied to a particular firm), G is the growth rate of the firm, and a is the rebate rate coefficient. In a diagram, plotting G on the vertical and R on the horizontal axis, (14) will be a straight line such as A in Figure 1. (The plan envisages no rebate payments at negative rates of growth. A therefore coincides with the G axis below the origin.)

It is assumed that the firm reacts according to a "reaction curve" of the form

$$(15) \qquad\qquad G = b_1R + b_2$$

which may be a line such as B in Figure 1.[10] (The fact that B cuts the G axis above the origin indicates that the firm will maintain some positive rate of growth even in the absence of subsidy payments.) If the firm starts with a rate of growth indicated by C, it will achieve a rebate rate shown by the horizontal coordinate of D, which will induce it to produce a rate of growth shown by E, and so on, until it finally reaches the equilibrium point F where the two lines intersect. If point C were below the horizontal axis (corresponding to a firm which is declining initially), the firm could either remain there and continue the decline after the introduction of the growth plan or it could jump to point F in one step. Clearly other possibilities exist as well. In any case, it is relevant for the operation of the growth plan to know the shape and position of line B.

The appropriate econometric model may contain the following two structural equations:

$$(16) \qquad a_{11}R_t + a_{12}G_t + a_{13}G_{t-1} + \ldots + a_{1,k+2}G_{t-k} \qquad\qquad = 0$$

$$(17) \qquad a_{21}R_t + a_{22}G_t \qquad\quad + a_{2,k+3}k_t + a_{2,k+4}R_{t-1} + a_{2,k+5}W = u_t$$

where R_t is the rebate rate in period t, k_t is the penalty tax rate in period t, G_t is the growth rate in period t and W is a summary representation of all the economic variables other than those arising from the operation of the growth plan. Equation (16) is the Government's reaction curve. It states that the re-

---

[10] A similar construction would be obtained by using the net payment rate $aG - k$ (rebate rate minus penalty tax rate) instead of the rebate rate. Figure 1 is illustrative and is not intended to suggest that reaction curve B is necessarily linear.

bate rate (applying to a firm) is some weighted sum of past and present growth rates. Equation (17) states that the growth rate achieved by the firm depends on present and past rebate rates, the penalty tax rate, and certain economic variables included under W. The variable u_t in Equation (17) is a random variable indicating the stochastic nature of this equation.[11]

The first task is to distinguish jointly determined and predetermined variables in the model.[12] Clearly G_t and R_t are jointly determined variables.

$$G_{t-1}, \ldots, G_{t-k}, R_{t-1}, k_t$$

are predetermined since they are either past values of jointly determined variables or are given constants such as k_t. W, being a summary for all other factors influencing the rate of growth, will contain some jointly determined variables such as current prices, wage rates, consumer expenditures, etc., and some predetermined ones such as the rate of growth prior to the introduction of the growth plan, government spending, and so on. To complete the structure, one would have to add as many structural equations as there are jointly determined variables encompassed by W. Only then can the structure determine a unique set of values for the jointly determined variables.[13] Any number of methods could then be utilized to determine statistically the values of the parameters in Equation (17), provided that observations on a sufficiently large sample of firms were available.

A self-liquidating growth plan. If the growth scheme were

---

[11] Note that no random error appears in Equation (16) since that equation holds by definition. This fact renders the present two-equation model formally analogous to the Haavelmo model. See W. C. Hood and T. C. Koopmans, *Studies in Econometric Method* (Cowles Commission Mono. No. 14; Wiley: New York, 1953), Ch. IV.

[12] Jointly determined variables are those which are determined within the model. Predetermined variables are given from outside the model.

[13] Inspection reveals that if we neglect W and consider Equations (16) and (17), the complete structure, the second equation is overidentified. Its parameters can then be estimated by a number of alternative methods.

to be operated in such a manner that the Government's re-ceipts from the penalty tax just cover the payments it is called upon to make on rebate account, one would have to know the tax and rebate rate structure that would achieve this.

It is a simple matter to show mathematically that a necessary and sufficient condition for the equality of tax and rebate pay-ments is given by

$$(18) \qquad\qquad a\overline{G} = k$$

where a and k have their usual meanings and where G is the average rate of growth in the economy.[14] The determination of the appropriate a and k is as follows. We choose a particu-lar value of a. This would determine a unique k by Equation (18) if $\overline{G}$ were known. $\overline{G}$, however, is itself a jointly determined variable in the system. Use therefore Equations (16) and (17) to determine the value of G_t for each firm and for each poten-tial value of the tax rate. In general one would expect to find that for a given a a higher k will result in a lower value of G. From the individual firms' growth rates the average rate of

---

[14] *Proof:* Let V_{it} be the value added of firm i in period t, R_{it} the rebate rate applying to the ith firm in the tth period and G_{it} the growth rate in value added for the ith firm in the tth period. Then

$$(19) \qquad\qquad \frac{V_{it} - V_{it-1}}{V_{it-1}} = G_{it}$$

$$(20) \qquad\qquad aG_{it} = R_{it}$$

The requirement that aggregate penalty tax and rebate payments be equal is expressed by

$$(21) \qquad\qquad a\sum_i G_{it}V_{it} - k\sum_i V_{it} = 0$$

It follows from Equation 21 that

$$(22) \qquad\qquad a\left(\frac{\sum\limits_i G_{it}V_{it}}{\sum\limits_i V_{it}}\right) = k$$

where the expression in parentheses is clearly the average rate of growth with value added weights.

growth corresponding to every value of k can be calculated and plotted as curve M_0 in Figure 2. For the given value of a, Equation (18) is plotted as N_0 in Figure 2. The intersection of M_0 and N_0 provides the correct value of k, that is the value which, together with the prespecified value of a will produce an average growth rate consistent with the self-liquidating requirement expressed by Equation (18).

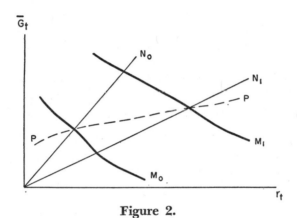

Figure 2.

At this stage in the procedure a is the only arbitrarily chosen parameter in the system. This parameter must now be chosen in such a manner that the average rate of growth achieved as a consequence of involving the self-liquidating features of the plan is equal to some target rate. As different values of a are chosen the M curve and the N curve both shift to, say, positions M_1 and N_1. An examination of the intersections of corresponding M and N curves (describing a locus such as PP) allows one in general to pick a value of a which both produces the desired average rate of growth and preserves the self-liquidating feature of the plan.

Next, consider how changes in the rebate rate coefficient affect the average rate of growth under the self-liquidating requirement.[15] The intuitive argument below utilizes the three-dimensional diagram in Figure 3, with the rebate rate R and the penalty tax rate k on the two horizontal axes, and the average rate of growth on the vertical axis.

The pairs of lines emanating from the $\overline{G}k$ plane represent the Government's (the A curves) and the economy's (the B curves) reaction curves at each possible level of k. Since we imposed the self-liquidating constraint expressed by Equation (18), a higher k corresponds to a higher a for given $\overline{G}$. Thus the successive Government reaction lines A_1, A_2, A_3 become less steep as one gets farther from the origin since (1) the slope of an A curve is $1/a$ and (2) k and a move together for given $\overline{G}$. It is not clear how the economy's reaction lines behave. It

---

[15] A mathematical derivation of the conclusions discussed below can be given as follows: Consider the system discussed in Section 2 and assume that it represents the aggregate production problem of the economy. Assume also that both a and k are allowed to change. Taking total differentials leads to the system of simultaneous equations

$$\begin{bmatrix} r_{11} & r_{12} \\ r_{12} & r_{22} \end{bmatrix} \begin{bmatrix} dM \\ dF \end{bmatrix} = \begin{bmatrix} 0 \\ [f_2 - 2(1 + G)]\, da + f_2\, dk \end{bmatrix}$$

Invoking the self-liquidating constraint $aG = k$ and substituting $da = dk/G$ into the previous equation gives

$$\begin{bmatrix} r_{11} & r_{12} \\ r_{12} & r_{22} \end{bmatrix} \begin{bmatrix} dM \\ dF \end{bmatrix} = \begin{bmatrix} 0 \\ (f_2 - 2)\left(1 + \dfrac{1}{G}\right) dk \end{bmatrix}$$

Hence
$$\frac{dM}{dk} = \frac{-r_{12}(f_2 - 2)\left(1 + \dfrac{1}{G}\right)}{\Delta}$$

$$\frac{dF}{dk} = \frac{r_{11}(f_2 - 2)\left(1 + \dfrac{1}{G}\right)}{\Delta}$$

Since $f_2 < 1$ and $\Delta > 0$, both derivatives are positive and output increases with a balanced budget increase in the tax rate and rebate rate coefficient.

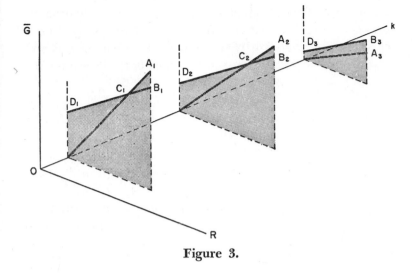

Figure 3.

is plausible that the points D_1, D_2, D_3 at which they emanate
from the $\overline{G}k$ plane lie closer and closer to the horizontal axis,
since, in the absence of a rebate rate, a higher penalty tax rate
will tend to reduce the rate of growth. It is also plausible that
the slopes of successive B curves are higher and higher. The
reason for this is that a given increase in R is likely to have a
greater boosting effect on $\overline{G}$ when k is large than when it is
small. From these considerations it cannot be shown unam-
biguously that the successive intersection points C_1, C_2, C_3
correspond to higher and higher levels of $\overline{G}$. It can be said,
however, that if the successive downward displacement of
points D_1, D_2, D_3 occurs in moderate steps, the successive intersections will lie on an ascending locus.

In conclusion, we consider some broad, general equilibrium
implications of the growth scheme. Partial equilibrium analysis led to the conclusion that the introduction of the growth
scheme will increase the output produced and the quantity of

factors hired by the firm. Since this conclusion was reached on the assumption that the firm can be considered in isolation, it must now be qualified by relaxing some of the assumptions. Specifically, we may relinquish the assumption of given product and factor prices without, however, abandoning the assumption that the average price level remains constant (as a result, perhaps, of over-all price stabilization policies by the monetary and fiscal authorities).

Since the introduction of the growth scheme places a premium on faster growth, firms' demand curves for factors of production will tend to shift to the right. Unless all factor supply curves are infinitely elastic, some changes in relative factor prices are likely to result. A firm which spends a large proportion of its budget on the factor F whose price has risen relatively highest and which, in the absence of relative price changes, would have purchased an additional x units of F will now find that the subsidy payments it would receive for maintaining a high rate of growth no longer compensate it for the reduction in operating profit. It will, therefore, not expand output as much as it would have if no factor price changes had occurred. It is even possible that the output of this firm diminishes, provided that other factors are not easily substitutable for factor F. Although the effect of the scheme on particular firms thus depends upon configuration of the elasticities of supply and demand for the various factors and products, the over-all effect of the scheme is still to stimulate the rate of growth. In general, the scheme is likely to exert a most favorable effect on those industries which have a great deal of excess capacity (where the marginal physical product of labor is fairly steady) and which face highly elastic supply curves for inputs.

SPECTRUM 🐚 PAPERBACKS

Other SPECTRUM BOOKS . . . quality paperbacks that
meet the highest standards of scholarship and integrity.

The American Assembly Series

Science and Technology Series

3   172